GETTING
UNSTUCK

GETTING UNSTUCK

ROBERT S. MCGEE
AND PAT SPRINGLE

WORD PUBLISHING
Dallas·London·Vancouver·Melbourne

Getting Unstuck: Help for People Bogged Down in Recovery
by Robert S. McGee and Pat Springle

Copyright © 1992
Rapha Publishing/Word, Inc.
Houston and Dallas, TX

First Printing, 1992

ISBN: 0–945276–32–X
Printed in the United States of America

Contents

◆

Acknowledgments

◆

WE HAVE WATCHED MANY PEOPLE struggle and grow through the process of emotional and spiritual healing. We have learned a lot from these people about grace, persistence, and character. In the tough decisions, day after day, they have been examples to all of us.
We also want to thank . . .

Sandy Ballard for designing and producing the manuscript;
Richard Price, Russ Rainey, Pete Kuiper, Wes Harbor, and Mark Baker for their ideas and insights; and
Stan Campbell for his editing expertise.

Foreword

$\blacklozenge$

When I first saw the title of this book, I was immediately reminded of an incident in my life. It happened when I was in my early twenties and studying to become a Civil Engineer in South Africa. I had just learned the rudiments of land surveying and was asked to go into a rather isolated part of the veld, some miles outside our town, to survey a parcel of land for a proposed road. I was rather excited. This was to be my first "solo" survey job.

Early in the morning I packed the four-wheel drive jeep I was to use, picked up my two surveyor aides whose jobs were to hold the survey rods, measure distances with tapes and so forth, and set out across the veld to find the starting point for the survey project. No roads. Just a compass to show me the direction.

It had rained the night before. Not just our Los Angeles type of rain, but African type of rain, by the buckets. The soil was soaked. There were many large "vlies" or stagnant pools of water that had turned the soil, rich in clay, into slippery quagmires, dangerous even for a four-wheel drive jeep.

So I kept saying to myself, *Be careful, watch out for bog holes.* The terrain was flat but with tall grass as is found on the high-veld of the Transvaal. I tried to steer clear of grass that looked too green—it was bound to signal a swamp area. I looked for higher ground, though it was so flat you couldn't tell high from low. *Be careful. Go slow. You can't afford to get stuck out here. No one will know where to find you.*

Then my worst fear befell me. Going quite slowly, I was in the middle of a marshy area before I realized it. The wheels spun and I DIDN'T MOVE.

Wait, be cool, I tried to reassure myself. *This jeep has a drive on all four wheels. It can literally float its way out of mud.* At least, that's what I had been told. Obviously just sales talk—because nothing I did budged that jeep. I WAS STUCK. Stuck in the mud. Down to the axle in mud. I didn't even want to step down from the jeep because I knew I would sink to my knees in sticky, black clay.

I sat there immobilized. I felt embarrassed. The two older African men who were my survey aides must have thought I was really dumb. They said nothing. I desperately wanted to be somewhere else. Since I couldn't, I thought I would try to be humble so as to look as good as possible. I had no choice. I had to apologize and ask for their advice. This was my first field trip, they had been on dozens. I was a green horn, they were seasoned pros. But I was the professional, they were mere laborers. I should have known better. Perhaps, I thought, they would know what to do.

They sure did! In three minutes we were out and moving again. The jeep had a winch on the front. I hadn't noticed it. One of the men looked around for a sturdy shrub on dry ground, attached the cable near the bottom, and the other man pushed the switch. Together with some low torque on the four drives we just sailed out of the quagmire like the sales pitch had promised. I was extremely thankful—though humbled.

This book is about that winch and we are like that jeep, stuck in the mud. Many of us are bogged down with long-buried emotional wounds and "unfinished" business from our childhoods. We feel handicapped by unhealthy defense mechanisms and in-effective strategies for coping with life's demands. We are literally *stuck* and don't know which way to go or how to get *unstuck.*

I cannot think of any better persons that Robert McGee and Pat Springle to show us how to get moving again. Like my two aides they point us to a "winch," or perhaps many winches, that can help pull us out of our mires of emotional mud and put us on drier ground where healing can take place. Without such help we would be stuck forever. Most of us are solidly entrenched in a morass of painful and dysfunctional relationships or handicapped by some pattern of self-destructive behavior. We have tried to navigate our lives, but the swamps are many and no sooner do we get out of one and we are in another.

Here we are shown how to get unstuck, and, more importantly, *stay unstuck*. What excites me about this book, more than its obvious professional quality, the sheer competence of the authors and the practical effectiveness of its guidance, is the fact that the winches they point us to are not anchored to some scrubby little tree in the vast veld of human experience. They are anchored to a Rock. It is a big Rock, an everlasting Rock, a Rock for all ages. It will never fail us. Again and again we are shown the relevance of God's resources in helping us overcome such swamps as bitterness, fear, shame, and grief. With God's help we can get unstuck. God can give us the courage to change ourselves and our circumstances, the boldness to take risks and abandon our crutches, the wisdom to analyze our problems, and the power to overcome our deep resistances and defense mechanisms.

God desires our wholeness. He is in the business of rebuilding broken lives and fostering emotional growth as much as spiritual growth, though I cannot separate the two in reality. But wounded people must take some responsibility to move themselves out of their broken and bogged-down state. You can sit there on your jeep if you want to. You're not going to go anywhere, and sooner or later you will drown in the mud of apathy. Or you can anchor your life to the Rock of Ages and with the help offered here begin to winch yourself out of your "stuck" state. My prayer is that you will join me in the adventure of getting unstuck.

ARCHIBALD D. HART, PH.D.
DEAN AND PROFESSOR OF PSYCHOLOGY
FULLER THEOLOGICAL SEMINARY
GRADUATE SCHOOL OF PSYCHOLOGY

CHAPTER

1

◆

The Blob
and
the Abyss

—Pat Springle

Perception is often an elusive creature. A clear knowledge of oneself is usually harder to develop than we expect. It seems that every time we convince ourselves we are finally seeing life with crystal clear vision, we eventually discover that our views are still warped and distorted. And sometimes it seems like the more we get involved in the painstaking process of gaining perception—about ourselves, our families, our emotions, and our behaviors—the more we *still* don't understand.

I speak from personal experience. I had been learning a lot about my own codependency. I had written on the subject. I had spoken at conferences and led groups. My life and relationships were much more fulfilling than ever. Yet something wasn't right. It seemed that the healthier I got, the greater my nagging sense that I hadn't dealt with something. I was setting more reasonable limits in relationships and enjoying the Lord and life more. My intense drive to succeed and please people was increasingly being replaced with a sense of peace, but still. . . .

As layers of denial, drivenness, facades, and fear were gradually stripped away, I became increasingly aware of deeper wounds. I talked to a close friend about how I felt, but I couldn't come up with any good descriptions or metaphors. The best I could define what I was feeling was "a big, black blob at the core of my life." After all I had learned . . . after all I had changed . . . after all I had grown . . . I still felt a sense of both confusion and shame.

We continued to talk. "It doesn't have any handles yet," I said. "It's just hurt, fear, and anger." He asked how I felt. "Hopeless, I guess. I can't do anything about it if I can't find the handles."

A DRIVE TO SUCCEED

Susan described her inner pain somewhat differently. She had been neglected by her workaholic father, and her emotionally crippled mother had looked to her for comfort. In effect, Susan became her mother's parent, taking responsibility for Mom's emotional state.

Susan learned to cope with her pain by "being the best." In high school she made good grades, played on the varsity tennis team, and was voted "Most Popular" in her class. In college, being the best became more difficult because the level of competition was higher, but she was still driven to succeed. Susan got a good job after graduation, and three years later she got married. Her relationship with her husband reflected her success goals. As a couple, they were always on the go, filling their lives with "fun and meaningful things." Even at church Susan was known as "somebody we can count on to get things done."

Yet as a sales representative in a highly competitive market, Susan could no longer outperform everyone else. She began to experience failure—more than she could handle.

Losing at the comparison game was a new experience for Susan. When she confronted this stark reality, she became depressed and withdrawn. Her exuberant confidence turned to despair. Her energy quickly withered into lethargy. I met her after she had been depressed for about a year. When I asked her to explain her childhood and her relationship with her parents, she told me the facts. Yet there was no hint of emotion as she spoke of being neglected by one parent and smothered by the self-pity and helplessness of the other. She matter-of-factly explained her rise to popularity in high school and college, her driven lifestyle, her superficial marriage, and her failure to excel at work.

Susan's tone sounded more like the six o' clock news than a description of a life filled with hurt and despair. There were no feelings expressed at all—just words.

Sensing that her denial was thick and hard, I asked, "Susan, what generally makes you angry?"

She answered confidently, "Nothing. I don't get angry. I guess I've grown past that." Then she sighed, "But I know something's wrong. I just don't know what it is."

"I've spent my life trying to be somebody . . . just wanting somebody to care about me . . ."

Several months of weekly discussions followed, and slowly—very slowly—Susan began to feel again. Then she became suddenly overwhelmed by the enormity of her pain. She sobbed, "I've spent my life trying to be somebody . . . just wanting somebody to care about me . . . but now I feel so empty, so alone, like I've fallen into an abyss with no bottom to it—and nobody with me to hold on to."

All of us want to love and be loved. But many of us have been so deeply wounded that we can't bear the pain. Like Susan, we can completely stuff our emotions inside. We can hide. We can cover the hurt with many layers of successes, escapes, compulsions, and reactions so we won't have to feel it. But it's still there.

ONIONS AND EGGS

Many of us need months (or years) involved in the healing process—dealing with layer after layer of destructive behaviors, strained relationships, and painful feelings—before we discover the stark reality of our own "blob" or "abyss." But that's what it takes to eliminate the seething anger and hurt we feel, and our desperate emptiness.

For example, when I speak about codependency and list its characteristics, many listeners tell me they haven't experienced loneliness. Almost universally, I find that these people are not far into the recovery process. They are by no means free. Often, they still feel indispensable to others, or they have so few limits that others easily control them.

But as they progress, they begin to grieve previous emotional losses. They begin to set limits. They identify relationships based on manipulation rather than love. They see how their "close relationships" have actually been utilitarian. Since their perceived value has always been based on performance, they are now gripped by the feeling of being abandoned, of being without connections, of being alone. People who experience this kind of recovery compare it to peeling an onion—removing layer after layer of defense mechanisms.

For others, the experience of emotional healing is more like breaking an egg. The stark reality of emptiness or of being emotionally attacked is felt very soon in the process. They feel overwhelmed, helpless, and hopeless. The shell cracks, then shatters, and all the repressed fear, hurt, and bitterness fall out at once.

WHERE WE'RE HEADED

This book focuses on the realities and complexities of long-buried emotional wounds, how defense mechanisms affect behavior, and the accompanying strains in relationships that result. We will see how abuse and neglect prevent our deepest needs from being met, and create a rogue's gallery of craving, fear, shame, and hatred—though these feelings may be so deeply buried that we may not be even remotely aware of them in our lives. But whether or not we know they are there, they profoundly affect our motivations, our relationships, thoughts, feelings, and behavior. They form the backdrop of every decision and every interaction.

The process is often baffling and difficult. Many of our usual "answers" are in reality a major part of the problems.

Continued denial doesn't solve the problem. Facing your own "blob" or "abyss" takes courage. The process is often baffling and difficult. Many of our usual "answers" are in reality a major part of the problem. We may discover that our values need to be radically changed, our perception of God and ourselves needs to be altered, and our very framework of making decisions needs to be replaced. We have to grieve our losses—sometimes enormously painful losses—and take responsibility for our lives. Someone has compared this process to "reaching down your throat, grabbing hold of your toenails, and pulling until you're turned inside out."

A few years ago, I told a friend, "I need to understand what's going on with me." He said, "Pat, you need to *feel* understood even more than you need to understand." Like many other statements from my wise friend, I had to ponder this one awhile, but I finally realized he was right. We need to know that somebody understands us. That bond with another person for whom we need not "perform" provides the foundation for growth and healing. Then we can increasingly understand ourselves and learn to relate to God and others in more healthy ways.

The purpose of this book is first to help you feel understood, and then to help you understand, to guide you to a healing environment, and to encourage you to persevere in the healing process.

How does God fit into this process? You may be surprised. Many of us think of God as harsh and cruel, or disgusted with us all the time. We feel that we can't possibly do enough to please Him, or that He simply doesn't care. We may believe that He has promised us a lot but hasn't delivered, so He can't be trusted. Whenever our perception of God is distorted, the tremendous guilt we feel in our relationships with Him is a significant part of the problem.

But when we step back and look at the major themes of the Bible, we see a God who is very different from the one many of us imagine. He is a God who comforts the hurting, who is near to the suffering, who helps people take responsibility for their behavior, and who is patient and kind even when we don't understand Him. This book will help you develop a more accurate perception of God and experience His love, kindness, and strength.

REFLECTION/DISCUSSION

1. Write a chronicle of your life. Take each period of time and describe important events which occurred, how others acted during and after these events, and how you felt and responded. You may want to divide the periods by significant events such as: Before Starting School; Before Parents' Divorce; High School Years; Early Adult Years; Years Before Marriage; etc. Before you start, ask God to help you remember events clearly so you can reflect on how the situations and the people affected you. Outline these periods and significant events below. Then on other paper, write out a more detailed chronicle of your life.

2. How do you feel as you reflect on what you have written?

3. Have you experienced a measure of healing for each of the wounds caused by others? Have you taken responsibility for your own behavior? If so, what factors have helped you?

4. Read Psalm 27:13–14. What do these verses tell us about our hope in the Lord?

2

◆

Why We Get "Stuck"

—Robert S. McGee

Aᴌᴍᴏsᴛ ᴇᴠᴇʀʏᴏɴᴇ ʜᴀs ᴘʀᴏʙʟᴇᴍs in achieving goals and establishing relationships. We all need healing from time to time. Yet some people never get started in the healing process. Others get started and make good progress for a while, but for some reason have their progress blocked at some point. They are "stuck." In fact, they may get stuck at several crucial points along the way.

Ability to identify the problem(s) can vary from person to person. Some know why they aren't making progress. One lady told me, "I just can't do it. It hurts too much to even think about my ex-husband abusing my daughter and me. Maybe someday. . . ."

But many of us have no idea why we aren't progressing. "I don't know what in the world is wrong with me," a man lamented. "I seemed to be doing better for a while, but now I'm going *backward*! I'm really disappointed in myself." This man's response is typical. He failed to grow at the pace he expected. And since he already had a poor self-concept, he focused the blame on himself. His shattered expectations led to feelings of failure, self-contempt, and severe discouragement.

Identifying and understanding roadblocks is a very important part of anyone's journey toward restoration. When we can see them, we can remove them or go around them, and our progress can continue. In this chapter, we will examine five common reasons why people get stuck in the process of emotional healing.

---

5 Reasons We Get "Stuck" in the Process of Emotional Healing

1 – We are not desperate enough for change.
2 – We are unwilling to take risks.
3 – We lack sufficient emotional support.
4 – We make a wrong analysis of the problem.
5 – We are unwilling to take responsibility.

REASON #1: WE ARE NOT DESPERATE ENOUGH FOR CHANGE.

People will not seek change in their lives until a sense of desperation overcomes their emotional inertia. No matter how much pain they have experienced, they develop elaborate coping mechanisms to help block it. Only when these mechanisms fail to protect them, or when additional pain overloads their defenses, does the anxiety level tend to escalate to the point that they seek help.

One common way to avoid pain is by *repression* of all hurt and anger. I know. I've done it. As a child I didn't know any constructive ways to process my pain, so I learned to "stuff it" and deny that I hurt at all. Repression seems like a useful way to cope at first, but it has long-lasting effects. It can make a person emotionally numb and mechanical. He may avoid some of painful feelings, but he also misses many pleasant emotions such as love, joy, and happiness.

Comparison is another method of negating the desperation for change in our lives. We keep up with how we compare to other people through a variety of "scoreboards."

Some of us have developed a "rules scoreboard." We categorize life into "to-do lists," governed by rigid systems and expectations for our behavior. If we do well enough . . . score high enough . . . if our performance meets an arbitrary, intrinsic score . . . we determine that we're doing okay.

Others have an "acceptance scoreboard." If we please enough people—or please a few certain people sufficiently—then that inner scoreboard registers a win. "I'm doing okay," a very depressed person told me. "A lot of people like me, so I must be doing all right." But "winning" on the scoreboard doesn't satisfy a deep longing to be loved. Many people give themselves a lot of points by being cute, funny, athletic, sensual, or daring, yet still feel "unconnected" to others. Paradoxically, they are popular and lonely at the same time. One woman explained in confusion and despair, "A lot of people think I'm their best friend, but I never let them know what I'm really thinking and feeling. I've played the game long enough and well enough to know how to make them think we're 'close,' but I also keep them away from the real me."

Still others of us have a "possessions scoreboard." They use things (cars, clothes, houses, vacations, etc.) to compare themselves with others. If they are doing "well enough," they have a vague, but fleeting, sense of security.

Most of us live with an eye on the "appearance scoreboard." If we look as good as this person and a little better than that one in terms of hair, complexion, figure, or weight, then the sense of desperation is held in check. A woman in a group shared, "All my life I've been in control of my appearance. I've gotten a lot of self-worth from my looks, but now I'm getting older and I'm so afraid of how I'm starting to look."

Excessive concern for appearance is certainly not limited to women. A man may be an astute executive, a good leader, a teacher in his church, and a loving father and husband. Yet his attention may be riveted to his growing bald spot, the flab around his waist he can't seem to lose, or complexion problems from his youth which continue to haunt him. He may be successful in business, but fearful and miserable inside.

Many people aren't even content to "look good" physically. In addition, they feel the need to be right in every decision, evaluation, and opinion. They fear that making a mistake will make them vulnerable, weak, and helpless, so they determine to *never* be wrong (even when they obviously are). Alice was one such person. She had an opinion about everything. Her drive for perfection had sharpened her perception and communication skills, and she could defend her positions against all comers. Yet when she was wrong, she would deny it or blame someone else for giving her incorrect information. It was never *her* fault.

For most people it is not a matter of being the *best* at fulfilling rules, winning acceptance, having possessions, or looking good. They only need to do "good enough" to avoid the pain of failure and rejection. Yet this pursuit consumes most of their lives.

In addition to repression and comparison, a third reason why someone's desperation level may never intensify is *low expectations*. Some people simply never expect much in terms of love, happiness, or health. A cycle develops where depression creates a mind-set of futility and hopelessness which then prolongs the depression. As a woman told me, "This is the best I can hope for. I've tried so hard and it's gotten me nowhere. Now I'm going to just accept the fact that life will never be any better."

Many influences can inhibit the sense of urgency and need in our lives. We are slow to get to a level of desperation that makes us want to take action. Yet even when we reach that point, fear can make us unwilling to take the risks which are necessary for change to occur.

Change—or even the prospect of change—necessarily involves risks which cause many . . . fears to surface.

REASON #2: WE ARE UNWILLING TO TAKE RISKS.

Wounded people are typically very fearful, though their fears may be deeply repressed. Change—or even the prospect of change—necessarily involves risks which cause many such fears to surface. Some become evident right away, some arise soon after perception begins, and others recur (for some people) throughout the healing process. These fears include:

The fear of feeling—Occasional eruptions of repressed emotions reveal a huge, sinister stockpile of hurt and anger waiting to be unleashed. Many of us are frightened of what we might feel if we allow those emotions to surface.

The fear of losing control—Emotions such as anger, hurt, self-pity, and so forth are frequently used to control others. These emotions give us power to manipulate people and a sense of security because we know how to use them to get what we want. We are afraid of losing that control and power.

The fear of admitting "I was wrong"—Many people feel too threatened to admit their mistakes. They reason that if they admit their sins and mistakes, they will be punished by not receiving love any more. These people can't see that the "love" they fear losing isn't genuine love at all. Instead of an unconditional love that includes respect and forgiveness, it is conditional and based on performance.

The fear of exposing "the family secret"—"If I talk about my family, how can I be sure you won't tell them?" Janice asked. She was horrified at the thought that her hidden knowledge might be revealed and that her "betrayal" would be exposed. She feared being abandoned by her family, her only support system (though it wasn't supportive at all). If that happened, she felt, she would have no one and nothing.

The fear of trusting—"I trusted the wrong people for so long," Dave told me, "I'm having a hard time trusting anybody now." As Dave risked trusting people in a support group, he began to open up and talk about his hurts and struggles. But after attending the group for several months, he overheard two group members talking about him outside the room. Dave was furious and devastated! Though one of these people had only referred to Dave's experience to illustrate a point, Dave felt betrayed. He stopped attending the group. It took Dave several months to overcome his bitterness and begin the process of learning to trust again.

REASON #3: WE LACK SUFFICIENT EMOTIONAL SUPPORT.

The fear of trusting others causes many people to try to deal with their emotional problems on their own or to let people know them only to a certain level, but no farther. One of the marks of emotional maturity is the willingness to allow people to know our true feelings and desires, so an environment of emotional support is vital to the healing process. As trust is developed, we are able to talk about our wounds, feel the long-repressed hurt and anger, experience comfort, and learn to be responsible for our behavior.

As we learn to trust people, our defenses come down bit by bit, and we can focus on others instead of constantly being on the defensive, afraid that someone will catch us, attack us, or abandon us.

This environment of support not only helps us to open up to others, but also allows us to listen. As we learn to trust people, our defenses come down bit by bit, and we can focus on others instead of constantly being on the defensive, afraid that someone will catch us, attack us, or abandon us.

We gradually learn who is trustworthy and who isn't. We may have trusted those who are not worthy of our trust, and the hurt of previous abuse or abandonment may have caused us to stop trusting *anyone*. But supportive, nurturing, strong relationships provide the opportunity to perceive people more correctly and find some who are worthy of trust.

Whenever people close to us continue to hurt us, we get stuck in the emotional healing process. For some, an insensitive spouse, child, or parent inflicts wound after wound. For others it might be an employer, friend, or neighbor who keeps them emotionally bruised and bleeding.

A person may experience a great deal of progress for a while, only to encounter someone who "presses his buttons" and jerks him back into old patterns of defensiveness, passivity, compulsion, or denial. Painful relationships are a fact of life for everyone. Until we learn to emotionally detach ourselves and continue to work through these relationships, they will continue to keep us stuck in our pain, anger, and fear.

Some people feel loved and accepted for the first time when they develop a relationship with a counselor or support group. These relationships can play a powerful positive role in emotional healing, but it's easy to get stuck at that point if people remain dependent on the counselor or group leader. Finding a nurturing, healing environment is a positive step, but it should lead to additional growth and healthy independence, not continued dependence.

REASON #4: We make a wrong analysis of the problem.

Most people do not have a clue as to the identity or extent of their root needs and problems. Consequently, they spend vast amounts of energy, time, emotions, and money on dealing with relatively superficial problems. Dr. Larry Crabb has stated that our "core wounds" are belonging, worthiness, and competency, but most people perceive other needs and try to fulfill them (*InsideOut*, NavPress). They believe that if they perform well enough, look good enough, or have enough acceptance, then they will be truly happy. When these things don't bring fulfillment, most people redouble their efforts instead of searching for a better source of satisfaction. For example:

- A person who is driven to succeed may conclude, *I must not be trying hard enough*, even though he is working 60 hours a week and staying compulsively busy at home as well.

- A lethargic, depressed person may conclude he has the latest popular "disease" instead of facing his repressed hurt and anger. (One recent "epidemic" has been hypoglycemia—a valid diagnosis for some people, but a condition that most physicians believe has been over-diagnosed.)

Others have done what they *thought* was right for years, only to discover that their behavior has been harmful instead of helpful. Jane told me, "For 30 years I have lived to serve my husband. I was told by a Bible teacher that I had to honor him or I would be in big trouble. He quoted Scripture and everything. I did all I could do to please my husband. When I hurt, I didn't talk about it. When he failed to pay the bills, I had to use the grocery money to pay them. I could tell you a lot more. . . . I was sure I was doing the right thing, you know, what God wanted me to do. But now I think I lost my identity and kept him from being responsible. I am so confused and so angry!"

The root problems we need to face are our shame, fear,

hatred, and the craving to find love and security. We may make a tremendous effort to grow, but if we fail to deal with these issues we will find only surface solutions for surface problems. Of course, deception is a major reason why we fail to analyze the problems correctly. We believe we are "on the right track" and we truly expect to achieve relief and growth. Then, when our expectations are unmet, we often feel even more distressed, discouraged, and betrayed.

When core issues are not addressed, people in the healing process often transfer their compulsions and other dysfunctions from one area to another. They, in effect, "swap addictions." For instance, some people who have been addicted to alcohol become addicted to going to meetings. As alcoholics, they irresponsibly neglected their families, and now they continue to neglect them, but in a different way. They now insist on going to meetings where they feel comfortable instead of rebuilding strained relationships at home.

A codependent wife may swap her compulsion to fix her husband's problems for a compulsion to fix other people's problems at church. If church people don't recognize the root problems in her life, she will continue her compulsions—and be praised for her "servant spirit."

People can stay stuck for years believing they are doing the "right thing" when, in fact, they are perpetuating their dysfunctions.

Of course, alcoholics who go to meetings and codependents who get involved in helping others at church are not *all* swapping addictions, but this danger is very real. People can stay stuck for years believing they are doing the "right thing" when, in fact, they are perpetuating their dysfunctions.

Though the Bible encourages Christians to be open and honest with God (Psalm 62:8) and with others (Ephesians 4:15), many believers feel it is ungodly to have any negative emotions. To be a "good Christian," they believe, means that they should not be angry, depressed, or hurt. They repress these feelings and deny the wounds which caused them.

This faulty and damaging perception of the Christian life is too often taught from the pulpit as a once-and-for-all condition of "complete sanctification." This theological view suggests that at some point (whether at conversion to Christianity or at a later lordship commitment) we become pure in our motives and actions. Complete purity is certainly a goal for which we should strive, yet we should not overlook the many biblical passages that refer to our constant struggles with the world, our sinful desires, and the devil's schemes. (See, for instance, Romans 8:12–13, Galatians 6:7–9, Eph. 4:22–24, and Phil. 2:12–13.) As hard as we try to be pure, we should keep in mind that *complete* purity will not be ours until we see God face to face (1 John 3:1–2).

Those who adhere to the view of here-and-now complete sanctification have a big problem with failure. Instead of accepting failure as part of the normal, fallen, human condition—even for believers—they conclude that either God isn't powerful enough or faithful enough to keep them pure. Or they believe that some deep, hidden, hideous sin has prevented their purity. They are then driven to the extremes of either denial ("There's nothing wrong! I didn't sin!") or depression ("There's something really wrong with God or me! It's hopeless!").

REASON #5: WE ARE UNWILLING TO TAKE RESPONSIBILITY.

Victims of neglect and abuse understandably and reflexively blame others for their wounds. However, many victims begin to assign blame for virtually everything wrong in their lives. They are blinded by bitterness, and the victim–mentality prevents them from admitting their own sins, experiencing forgiveness, and in turn forgiving others who have wronged them. They focus blame on others in an attempt to punish them.

Many of us cope with dysfunction in our families by becoming care-takers. We compulsively fix others' problems, hoping to be appreciated for our efforts. But such preoccupation with the needs of others makes us overly responsible for them, and we expect or demand that others will reciprocate and meet our needs. Though we hate to admit it, we are irresponsible, unwilling to make the choices to take care of ourselves and to live healthy, balanced lives.

We need someone to trust before we can feel safe enough to admit our failures and sins.

Again, trust is a major factor in developing responsibility. We feel threatened to admit that we have failed to be responsible for ourselves, especially if we have prided ourselves on helping others. We need someone to trust before we can feel safe enough to admit our failures and sins. The anger generated in blaming others provides the power to keep going. But in a safe relationship we can begin to admit that we, too, have been wrong . . . we, too, have sinned . . . and we, too, need forgiveness. We learn to trade the power of blaming others for the power of being whole, strong, and forgiving.

OTHER FACTORS

Many other factors that contribute to getting us stuck somewhere in the healing process stem from our relationships with group leaders or the type of counseling we receive. Some of these include:

- The ego of the counselor or group leader may be stroked by someone's dependency on him for growth, so the person is subconsciously kept in a dependent role instead of discovering independence and maturity.

- The counselor or leader might fail to recommend other assistance. If the leader has codependent tendencies of his own, he may feel indispensable to others and refuse to admit when more intensive therapy or help is needed for the person in the process.

- New trends in "pop" psychology influence some group leaders or counselors. They become enamored with the latest "rabbit trails" instead of being sure that core issues are addressed with biblically sound psychological principles. While some current theories might provide helpful new insights, many others will get people off track.

- The artificial setting of an office may not provide the counselor with enough perception about the person's real-life responses and relationships. Additional support groups or meaningful friendships can provide important adjuncts to the counseling process.

- One short period each week (of personal counseling or in a group) may not provide enough time for a person to uncover deeply repressed emotions, to express them, and then "get pulled together" to go back to his daily routine. Appointments with counselors can be scheduled to give a longer time to reflect, express, and grieve. Groups are usually held at night and have less of a time constraint than appointments during the day.

Obviously counseling is profitable, and it can be an integral part of the healing process. Yet some counselors and groups are better than others. We need to be aware of potential pitfalls and difficulties so we can avoid them as much as possible.

GETTING UNSTUCK

All of us get stuck from time to time. We are imperfect people in an imperfect world seeking help from imperfect counselors and mentors. Our wounds can be deep and severe. To expect perfection after getting a little help is quite unrealistic, but it is possible to get unstuck more quickly and to avoid getting stuck so frequently.

Section 1 of this book will describe the root problems which we all need to deal with as we grow and heal. Section 2 explains the solutions for these problems, and Section 3 illustrates the process of growth.

As a preview of the solution and the process, here is a list of the essential elements of getting unstuck:

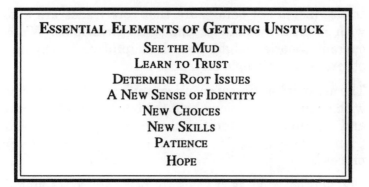

See the mud—That's what this chapter has been all about. The more clearly we can see the quicksand, the easier it is to avoid it. And if we find ourselves stuck from time to time, we can understand how we got that way and take steps to get going again.

Learn to trust—Dysfunctional relationships play a major role in causing both our pain and our sinful choices. But relationships with nurturing people provide an environment where we can learn to trust. Then we become willing to risk openness and honesty, and we learn to talk, feel, and choose.

Determine root issues—Instead of "spinning our wheels" and getting more depressed or driven when we fail to make substantial progress, we can learn to identify the root issues in our lives and apply the proper solutions to them.

A new sense of identity—Most of us have an "identity crisis." We try to be somebody we're not because we're afraid we won't be accepted for who we are. But the unconditional love, forgiveness, and acceptance of God can become real to us as we see these qualities modeled by other people and receive them for ourselves.

New choices—As we become more perceptive, we will be able to see many more choices in our lives. We learn to choose truth over deception, love over manipulation, and health and balance over dysfunctional behaviors.

New skills—We will learn to process our thoughts and feelings in order to make good choices. Also, we will learn to communicate our choices in positive, productive ways.

Patience—We need realistic expectations as we go through the healing process. Most of us "want it over with—*now!*" But years of misperception, mistrust, and misguided behaviors don't vanish in a flash.

Hope—One of the most important changes will be in our perception of God. We may have seen Him as harsh or uncaring, a tyrant or an impotent old man, but we will learn to see Him as both loving and powerful. He is the one true source of hope. Our hope is rooted in the expectation that God won't abandon us and that He will work in our lives to bring freshness and purpose.

The hope of the authors is that:

> [God] would grant you, according to the riches of His glory, to be strengthened with power through His Spirit in the inner man;
> So that Christ may dwell in your hearts through faith; and that you, being rooted and grounded in love,
> May be able to comprehend with all the saints what is the breadth and length and height and depth,
> And to know the love of Christ which surpasses knowledge, that you may be filled up to all the fulness of God.
> Now to Him who is able to do exceeding abundantly beyond all that we ask or think, according to the power that works within us,
> To Him be the glory in the church and in Christ Jesus to all generations forever and ever (Ephesians 3:16–21).

REFLECTION/DISCUSSION

1. Most of us try to "prove" our worth in various ways, including success, prestige, respect from friends, money, power, intellect, or special skills. Which of these have you used to gain a sense of value? How have you used them?

2. What are some results of trying to prove your worth in terms of your self-esteem, relationships, lifestyle, finances, etc.?

3. This chapter describes several reasons why people get "stuck."
   Review the chapter and describe to what extent each of these
   reasons has blocked your healing process:

   • Not Desperate Enough for Change

   • Unwilling to Take Risks

   • Lack of Emotional Support

   • Wrong Analysis of the Problem

   • Unwilling to Take Responsibility

   • Other Factors

4. Growth and healing result from acknowledging God's enablement and taking responsibility for ourselves. Read Philippians
   2:12–13. Describe how God's enablement and your responsibility are both depicted in this passage.

5. What do you need to let God do for you? What do *you* need to
   do to facilitate your growth?

Section One

———◆———

3

◆

Mirrors

—Robert S. McGee

I LOVED GOING TO THE FAIR when I was a child. All the kids at school would talk about it for weeks.

"Do you remember last year's fair? That fat lady was *huge!*"

"Yeah, I won a parakeet at the ring toss . . . but it died a couple of days later. You think that being dyed purple had anything to do with it?"

"My Dad got really mad 'cause he spent ten dollars trying to win a teddy bear at the baseball throw, but he never knocked all three bottles down . . . and another guy did it on the first try."

"I like the Round-a-Bout. I rode it six times straight!"

"Yeah, right! When I rode it, the guy next to me threw up and it got all over everybody!"

Ah, yes. I have such fond memories of going to fairs! One of my personal favorites was "The Haunted House," which always had a room full of those crazy mirrors. One made me look really tall. Another one, short and fat. I especially liked the one that made you look fat in the middle with long, skinny legs and neck. My buddies and I would jump up and down to make different parts of our bodies take on different shapes. We thought it was great fun!

Some psychologists, notably Virginia Satir (*New Peoplemaking*, Science and Behavior Books, 1988), have found that parents act as mirrors for their children. A child determines things such as his value, abilities, and worth as a person by his parents' attitudes and actions toward him. If parents are loving and kind, provide a safe home environment, and encourage growth toward individual responsibility, then they are very good mirrors of a child's worth. Generally, children in these homes grow up with a healthy sense of identity, able to give and receive love, and willing to take responsibility for life's tasks.

But like carnival mirrors, parental "mirrors" can be distorted. The more distorted the mirror, the more distorted the image. If the child perceives a reflection of being unsafe, unlovable, or worthless, he begins to develop problems with his identity, relationships, and level of responsibility (either too much or too little).

There are not just two kinds of parental mirrors: good or bad. They vary in type along a broad continuum. Some reflect very positively in some areas but negatively in others. The parents' reflection to the child can be affected by factors such as the sensitivity of the child, the child's relationships with other relatives and friends, health factors, and sociological factors. Yet parents provide the most powerful and consistent reflection of a child's value. The reason we thought the mirrors in the "Haunted House" were funny was that we had other accurate mirrors with which to compare our reflections. But if someone has only one distorted mirror to look into every day, he may believe that it is himself—not the mirror—which is distorted.

SOCIOLOGICAL FACTORS

This chapter will focus on the powerful role of our parents in shaping our lives, but we need to see this vital relationship in the context of sociological factors. Recently two studies have revealed the reality of how much more pressure is placed upon parents and children today compared to only three decades ago.

A teachers' survey asked, "What are the biggest problems in school?" The list the teachers rated 30 years ago in this survey is compared to a current teachers' survey:

30 Years Ago		Today	
1.	Chewing gum in class	1.	Drug abuse
2.	Not putting trash in the trash can	2.	Teen pregnancy/ sexual diseases
3.	Using bad language	3.	Vandalism
4.	Dressing inappropriately	4.	Aggressive/assaultive behavior
5.	Cheating	5.	Stealing

The stark contrast in this teachers' survey is confirmed in a study of lifestyles reported in H. Stephen Glenn and Jane Nelsen's book, *Raising Self-Reliant Children in a Self-Indulgent World*.[1] Even a cursory analysis of this study shows that enormous shifts have occurred in the family structure, the amount of interaction, and responsibilities faced by family members.

Characteristics	Norm 1930	Norm 1980
Family interaction	High	Low
Value system	Homogeneous	Heterogeneous
Role models	Consonant	Dissonant
Logical consequences	Experienced	Avoided
Inter-generational associations	Many	Few
Education	Less	More
Level of information	Low	High
Technology	Low	High
Non-negotiable tasks	Many	Few
Family work	Much	Little
Family size	Large	Small
Family dominant	Extended	Nuclear
Step/Blended/Single parent families	Few (10–15%)	Many (35–42%)
Class size (K–12)	18–22	28–35
Neighborhood schools	Dominant	Rare

In *Against the Night*, Charles Colson describes two insidious influences in our culture—individualism and relativism. In the urge to "find ourselves," our society has made man the center of the universe, distorting values, undermining truth, and destroying relationships. Of the plight of the family, Colson writes:

> Fragmented families and rootless youth are not confined to the inner city, of course. The crisis reaches every part of our society. Who hasn't seen the packs of mall orphans cruising shopping centers to avoid returning to homes shattered by divorce, neglect, or abuse? Each year about two million young people between the ages of thirteen and nineteen attempt suicide, and between 1950 and 1977 the suicide rate among adolescents quadrupled for males and doubled for females. What drives our youth to such horrifying lengths? Morally impoverished, groping for love and direction, the children [sic] find evil substitutes in all the wrong places.[2]

DISTORTED MIRRORS–DISTORTED LIVES

Sociological factors play a significant, if often undetected, role in relationships, but children don't care about sociology. They don't respond to surveys and studies. They only know about their immediate relationship with their parents. They respond to a hug or a glare, a word of affirmation or statement of disgust. Children have no objectivity to discern their parents' strengths and weaknesses. A child instinctively trusts that his parents are always right, so when parents communicate anger or apathy, the child concludes: There's something wrong with *me*!

Dysfunction in families is widely varied in magnitude and type. Variables are almost infinite, but we can at least put handles on some of these dysfunctions so we can know how to respond. As a friend says, "You can't change what you can't see." We will briefly analyze some of the more common dysfunctions, all of which are types of emotional abuse, defined as *any word or feeling which does not communicate love and respect*. The focus here is on parent-child relationships, but these same dysfunctions can occur in every other relationship—with a spouse, friend, employer, and so on.

SOURCES OF EMOTIONAL PAIN

VERBAL ABUSE   PHYSICAL ABUSE

SEXUAL ABUSE   PHYSICAL NEGLECT

EMOTIONAL NEGLECT   SMOTHERING

DOMINATING   MIXED MESSAGES

DOUBLE MESSAGES   ROLE REVERSALS

INTERNALIZED BLAME

VERBAL ABUSE

Perhaps the most common type of emotional pain comes from verbal abuse, and virtually all other types include a verbal element.

- "Mother would yell at me when I did anything wrong."

- "I could see Dad's anger boil, and then he would explode and cuss me out."

- "Mom laughed when my brother called me names: 'Stupid,' 'Dummy,' 'Jackass.' I'm not sure which hurt worse, the names or my mother's laughing."

- "My Dad could never be wrong. Anytime we argued, he had to win. We'd argue for hours sometimes, but after a few years, I just gave up and quit trying."

Verbal abuse is usually thought to be an outward expression of disgust, anger, and disrespect. But the absence of communicated love and respect is another form.

- "When I got hurt, mother's lips tightened and she wouldn't say a word. All I wanted was to hear her say, 'I'm sorry, son.' That would have been enough."

- "When my folks got angry at me, Dad would pick up the paper or a book to read and shut me out. Mom went to her room for a while. When she came out, she acted like nothing had happened."

PHYSICAL ABUSE

Beatings, tortuous pinching, or excessive corporal disciplines wound a child more emotionally than physically. Though the body may hurt from such abuse, the spirit is *crushed* because the implication of such treatment is that the child is worse than worthless. He feels like the cause of the parent's problems, which are so great they are uncontrollable.

- "Dad spanked me until I was 14 years old," a young woman tearfully related. "He got so angry . . . he grabbed me and hit me so hard. . . ."

- "I guess my father knew he shouldn't hit me, so when he got mad at me he held my face in his hands and pressed real hard. It hurt, but I guess he didn't feel as guilty about that as he would have about spanking."

- "I don't know why he did it. Almost every night I could hear his heavy footsteps coming up the stairs. I tried to hide under my bed or in my closet, but he found me. Usually he hit me in the back so nobody would know. For a long time I was sure my mother didn't know about it because she never said anything or stopped him or anything . . . but she *had* to hear him hit me. She *had* to hear me cry."

Many children of alcoholics or drug abusers can describe the violent explosions and beatings they endured. Of course, spouses may suffer this same treatment. Some outbursts may not be directed at the spouse or child, but the violence is still abusive and destructive. For instance, one man told me, "I remember my father getting so mad that he picked up a chair and threw it through a window. That only happened a few times, but it really scared me."

Withholding appropriate physical contact is another form of physical abuse.

- "My Dad never held me. I never sat in his lap. One time I tried to hold his hand. . . . It was stiff, and then he pulled it away."

- "I was locked in my room for hours at a time . . . sometimes whole days. Mom took the key. If I crawled out the window, my parents beat me, so most of the time I just waited. I felt so alone."

- "Dad was very affectionate with me until I began to develop as a woman. Then he stopped. He stopped completely. All at once he was cold toward me. I felt so confused and hurt and lonely. I think I needed him then more than ever, but. . . . It hurt really bad."

SEXUAL ABUSE

In their book, *Beyond the Darkness* (Rapha Publishing/ Word, Inc., 1992), Cynthia A. Kubetin and James D. Mallory, Jr., M.D. describe the tragic personal violation of sexual abuse. As a victim herself, Cynthia knows not only the horror of the act, but the deep and recurring sense of filthiness, shame, and hatred that result. Harry Schaumburg, D.Min., and I have defined sexual abuse as, "any sexual activity, either verbal or physical, engaged in without consent, which may be emotionally or physically harmful and which exploits a person in order to meet another person's sexual or emotional needs. The person does not consent if he or she cannot reasonably choose to consent or refuse because of age, circumstances, level of understanding and dependency or relationship to the offender."[3] Examples are rampant.

One pre-teenage girl felt lonely and unaccepted. A 40-year-old male neighbor invited her to visit him, and he showed her pornographic magazines. Though she "felt dirty," she enjoyed his attention and continued her visits. After two years, he began fondling her sexually.

Another woman related that her father's sexual advances when she was ten made her feel "special" at first, but soon she felt dirty and ashamed. He told her not to tell "their secret," and as she proved her trustworthiness, his advances progressed from fondling to masturbation to intercourse. But she kept her secret for years.

Other forms of active sexual abuse include rape, being the unwilling object of voyeurism, parents' inappropriate dress, and forced sex in marriage. Sexual abuse has also become more widely known in association with cult rituals in recent years. Horror stories of human sacrifices, animal sacrifices, and sexual orgies are shocking. Relationships in these cults are dehumanized. Polarities are reversed. Good is bad; bad is good; love is hate. Sexual acts are reduced to brutal, animal behavior devoid of warmth and intimacy.

And while it is not as damaging, another sexually abusive behavior is parental passivity in regard to discussing sex. Parents may not even want to mention sex because they feel embarrassed or ashamed about their own sexuality. Yet such avoidance implicitly communicates that all sex is dirty and wrong, and it distorts the child's view.

PHYSICAL NEGLECT

The absence of one or both parents through death, divorce, or workaholism leaves an emotional void in a child's life. Many single parents try desperately to fill that void—some more success-fully than others.

- "My mother died when I was six. Dad spent as much time with us as he could, but my grandmother raised me. I know she loved me, but I sure wish Mom hadn't died. . . . I miss her so much."

- "The divorce happened when I was in high school, but that wasn't the problem. The problem was all the yelling and hatred all those years before then. I wanted them to stay together so bad. Sometimes I acted sick so they would stop fighting with each other and give me some attention."

- "My Daddy wanted nice things, and he wanted my Mom to have nice things, too. He worked hard to get them . . . real hard. I don't remember him much when I was growing up. He worked until 7:00 or 8:00 six days a week. On Sunday he was so tired and grouchy I didn't want to be around him. I think he drank some, too."

EMOTIONAL NEGLECT

A parent may live in the home with the children, but still not provide emotional support. Emotional neglect typically occurs when a deeply wounded person focuses on his own needs and is unable to give attention to anyone else.

- "After the divorce, my mother was devastated. She withdrew into a shell. She had lost her husband, I know, but I was only twelve years old and I had lost my father! She came out of her depression about three years later, but by then. . . ."

- "I think my father was afraid of me—at least that's how he acted. He didn't seem interested in what I did at school or anything. Oh, he got excited about my brother: his baseball games, football, all that kind of stuff, but he didn't seem too interested in me at all."

SMOTHERING

At the other extreme of neglecting children is smothering them: providing *too much* attention, control, and direction. These parents feel threatened by the child's errors—or even potential errors. The child's failure would reflect negatively on their own fragile self-esteem, so they do all they can to prevent it. Perhaps they experienced the same kind of control, or maybe they were neglected and their controlling nature is a reverse reaction. Whatever the cause, smothering a child steals his self-confidence, spontaneity, and creativity.

- "I never had a problem my mother couldn't fix. She hovered over me like a hen over her chick. When I was hurt, she knocked herself out to comfort me. I thought I was a prince! She thought she was really helping me, I guess, but now I realize I expect somebody to bail me out of every problem."

- "My mother wouldn't let me breathe without telling me exactly how it ought to be done—then giving me a detailed analysis of every inhale and exhale. It got a little old."

- "I felt that I couldn't do anything right. No matter how well I did, it wasn't good enough. Even when I played with my friends, my father analyzed and criticized everything I did. He said he was trying to help me."

Frequently, smothering parents tell a child that they want him to be independent, but then they criticize him when he does something differently than they would. They talk about freedom, creativity, and affirmation, but the child experiences the opposite.

Author Garrison Keillor tells this story:

Our Sunday School class learned *Joy to the World* for the
Christmas program. You asked me to sing it for the Aunts
and Uncles when they came to dinner. I said, "No, please."
You said, "Yes, please."
I said, "No."
You said, "Someday when I'm dead and in my coffin,
maybe you'll look down and remember the times I asked
you to do things and you wouldn't."
So I sang, terrified of them, and terrified about your
death, and you stopped me halfway through; you said,
"Now, come on, you can sing better than that."
A few years later when I sang the part of Curly in
Oklahoma! and everybody else said it was wonderful,
you said, "I told him for years he could sing, and he
wouldn't listen to me."
But I did listen to you and that's most of my problem.
Everything you said went in one ear and down my spine.
Now you call me on the phone to ask, "Why don't you ever
call us? Why do you shut us out of your life?"
So I start to tell you about my life. But you don't want to
hear it. You want to know why I didn't call. I didn't call
because I don't need to talk to you anymore. Your voice is
in my head, talking constantly from morning until night.
I keep my radio turned on, but I still hear you, and I will
hear you all my life, until the day I die, when I will hear
you say, "I told you."[4]

DOMINATING

Usually those of us with smothering parents know they
think they are doing it for our good. But some of us had dominating,
authoritarian parents whose word was law.

One lady commented, "To disagree with Dad is to call into
question a divine principle—with the same calamitous consequences." She wasn't allowed to have her own opinions, unless of
course she agreed with him. Yet people in the community looked at
them as a "model family" and remarked about how "well-behaved"

the children were. The parents and children spent time together (as the father chose the time and place), they were very active in church, and they espoused conservative biblical and political doctrines (echoing Dad's opinions). It was a shock years later in the church and community when both children were in counseling, the son for his seething bitterness and the daughter for her depression and panic attacks. There was no mention of the mother. She still did what she was told.

MIXED MESSAGES

Each parent in many (if not most) families subconsciously seeks to balance or cover for the other one, which produces decidedly mixed messages for the children. The father may be a neglecting workaholic; the mother may smother. The father may be verbally abusive; the mother may be withdrawn, hurt, and needy. The father may be a controlling, rescuing codependent; the mother may be harsh and dominating.

People who have grown up in these families often tell me that their parents "balanced each other," but the children's lives don't reflect balance. More often they reflect hurt, shame, bitterness, and denial.

DOUBLE MESSAGES

Mixed messages are different communications by two separate parents. Double messages are different communications by the same person. Sometimes children hear verbal expressions of "I love you," "I respect you," or "I know you're trying your best." But the parent's tone of voice and facial expressions scream, *You're a jerk! Why would anybody trust you! You're a failure, and you always will be!*

Studies show that only seven percent of verbal communications consist of the actual words. Thirty-seven percent is conveyed by the tone of voice, and 56 percent by facial expressions.

Another form of double messages occurs when a person dramatically changes his method of communication. For instance, one man explained how his mother alternated between neglecting him and smothering him. Her Jekyll and Hyde communication left him emotionally devastated, insecure, and unable to build relationships because he was afraid to get close to anyone.

ROLE REVERSALS

When a parent faces severe emotional problems due to wounds from childhood, a divorce, death, illness, or some other difficulty, he may be unable to attend to the child's emotional needs. In these cases, the child may assume a parental role in the relationship. He comforts the hurting parent, takes responsibility to make the parent happy and productive, and assumes control. But this role reversal destroys the child's normal developmental process. He may act "grown up" in his relationship with his parents, but his needs for nurturing, security, freedom, and slow assimilation of responsibility remain unmet.

Trust is the foundation of future emotional and relational development.

Trust is the foundation of future emotional and relational development. Children don't decide to trust their parents; they do so instinctively. To the degree parents prove to be trustworthy, the child gains a sense of security. In these early years, the child expects the parents to tell him who he is—whether he has value and is acceptable, and on what they base their opinions.

As the child grows, the parents' role is to develop the child's perception and ability to make choices—to empower him to establish his own identity, personality, and behavior. An important result of this process is that the child learns who is trustworthy and who is not. Without this learned ability, he is doomed throughout life to trust those who are not worthy of his trust (and be perpetually manipulated) or to distrust everyone and remain isolated and alone. If the child is not encouraged and empowered to develop identity and perception, he will continue to look to others to give him a sense of value. He will be compelled to please, driven to succeed, or forced into passivity to avoid the risk of failure and rejection.

Dr. Dan Allender explains the relationship of trust and shame:

> Trust is a giving of our soul to another with the hope that we will not be harmfully used. Such trust invests in another the power to determine whether or not we are acceptable and desirable. When trust, defined as an empowering of another to determine our desirability and worth, is absent, shame is usually not experienced.[5]

Wendy told me, "When I was growing up, my mother dominated me. She told me when to brush my teeth, how to wash the car, what friends to have, how to smile . . . you name it! Everything I did was evaluated and critiqued. I never developed a sense of inner strength, so I always looked to others' approval to give me a sense of identity. I lived in fear that someone wouldn't appreciate me, and that fear drove me to do all I could to please people—then I gave up and rebelled. The fear of being rejected was a driving force in my life, just as much as real rejection. I guess I never developed a sense of who I really was."

The same result came from exactly the opposite situation. Rich's mother was very disinterested in him. "I never knew if I was doing well because I never got any feedback. When I brought home my report card, whatever I had done was okay with Mom and Dad. They never taught me how to do anything, so I hung around with other kids in the neighborhood—until they needed to go spend time with their folks. Now I look back and I really see that I longed to be valued. I trusted my parents to give me a sense of identity, and their neglect told me that I was worthless. Even since, I've desperately wanted affection and acceptance. I'm afraid that I won't get it, and even the slightest snub is terribly painful for me."

INTERNALIZED BLAME

Parents in these families may be driven by fear of failure or emotionally shackled by wounds suffered from their own parents. Very few parents intend to hurt their children. They try to do the best they can, but they are usually only too aware of their failures. Until someone has the perception and courage to change, abuse and neglect will continue from generation to generation (either duplicated in the same way or in the form of some opposite, or at least different, dysfunction).

. . .When the parents are out of control the child usually assumes, Something must be wrong with *me*!

One of the most tragic elements of these dysfunctions is the child's internalization of blame. As we mentioned earlier, when the parents are out of control the child usually assumes, something must be wrong with *me*! He internalizes the blame and represses the hurt, anger, and fear because he has no secure place and no safe people to talk to.

The combination of unmet needs, internalized blame, and repressed painful emotions produces a craving for love, a fear of being hurt again, a sense of shame for being so worthless, and a hatred for those who have wounded him—all covered over and explained away by elaborate defense mechanisms and coping devices so when he is asked how he's doing, he can say, "Just fine!"

Our goal is not to blame parents for all our problems. We do need to assign appropriate responsibility with the intention of forgiving anyone responsible. But to forgive an offense, we must come to grips with the reality—perhaps the horrible reality—of it. If our parents have hurt us, we don't want to thoughtlessly excuse them. Nor do we want to despise them. Forgiveness is a far preferable response that provides us the freedom to go on with our lives.

God instituted the family so parents would be the primary expression of His love, grace, and strength to children. But some of us experienced deep wounds at the hands of those sanctioned with the responsibility to protect and provide.

A friend has described how hard it is to be objective about the pain his parents caused him. They fought early in his life, then divorced. His mother needed a husband, so he became her emotional confidant. His father ridiculed him. Yet in spite of his unmet needs and deep hurts, he explained how much he wanted his parents to love him. He has not given up on his hope that they will somehow do *now* (when he is 40) what they didn't do when he was four. "Can you ever remove the power of a parent?" he asked.

My friend is not alone in his feelings. Adult children who are willing to talk about their pasts frequently find much in common. And they are beginning to band together in groups such as Adult Children of Alcoholics, Adult Children of Divorce, Adult Children of Dysfunctional Families, and so forth. These groups can do much to alleviate years of accumulated confusion, frustration, anger, and loneliness.

In the next four chapters, we will examine root causes of our pain and dysfunctions. These issues are also major factors of our getting stuck—and staying stuck—in the healing process. If we can feel that others understand us, and if *we* can understand, then we will be much more likely to find our way to personal wholeness and healthy relationships.

REFLECTION/DISCUSSION

1. Like the proverbial "frog in the kettle," how have you been affected by changing sociological factors without being aware of them?

2. What one changing sociological factor seems to affect you the most? Why?

3. Describe in detail the frequency and the severity of your experience with these sources of emotional pain. (Use more paper if necessary.)

    Verbal Abuse

    Physical Abuse

    Sexual Abuse

Physical Neglect

Emotional Neglect

Smothering

Dominating

Mixed Messages

Double Messages

Role Reversals

Internalized Blame

4. We often have difficulty analyzing the messages our parents
    gave us. As objectively as possible, write out the messages
    your parents communicated to you about yourself, themselves,
    and God. You may want to do this for significant periods of
    your life if one or both parents died or if their communication
    changed. For instance, a father may be abusive before a
    divorce, but absent and neglectful after it. Put your name in
    each blank and complete the thought.

YOUR FATHER'S MESSAGES TO YOU
During your early years: _____, you were . . .

During your middle years: _____, you were . . .

Today: _____, you are . . .

YOUR MOTHER'S MESSAGES TO YOU
During your early years: _____, you were . . .

During your middle years: _____, you were . . .

Today: _____, you are . . .

YOUR SPOUSE'S MESSAGES TO YOU
During your early years: _____, you were . . .

During your middle years: _____, you were . . .

Today: _____, you are . . .

YOUR CHILDREN'S MESSAGES TO YOU
During your early years: _____, you were . . .

During your middle years: _____, you were . . .

Today: _____, you are . . .

(Note: If memories of abuse occur, go to your pastor or a Christian counselor for help. These memories—and those still buried in your mind and heart—greatly affect your motives, self-concept, and relationships. Seek help so you can experience God's comfort, love, and strength.)

5.   We may tend to assume that God is like our parents, but we might be very wrong. Read Psalm 145. Compare and contrast your parents (or spouse) with God.

According to Psalm 145, God is:

My parents were (are):

[1] H. Stephen Glenn and Jane Nelsen, Ed.D., *Raising Self-Reliant Children in a Self-Indulgent World* (Rocklin, CA: Prima Publishing and Communications, 1989), pp. 30–31.

[2] Charles Colson, *Against the Night* (Ann Arbor: Servant, 1989), pp. 74–75.

[3] Robert S. McGee and Harry Schaumburg, *Renew: Hope For Victims of Sexual Abuse* (Houston, TX: Rapha Publishing, 1990), p. 5.

[4] Garrison Keillor, as quoted in *Raising Self-Reliant Children in a Self-Indulgent World,* written by H. Stephen Glenn and Jane Nelsen, Ed.D. (Rocklin, CA: Prima Publishing and Communications, 1989), p. 88.

[5] Dr. Dan B. Allender, *The Wounded Heart: Hope for Adult Victims of Childhood Sexual Abuse* (Colorado Springs, CO: NavPress, 1990), p. 54.

4

◆

Craving for Love

—Pat Springle

Bill had been in a codependency small group for about a year and a half. During that time, he had grown a lot. Having climbed to a top position in his company, he realized that his entire life had become characterized by a tremendous drive to succeed. So had his relationships. His quick mind and ability to "read" others' expressions generally gave him the upper hand in conversations. He knew what he needed to say to win approval. A lot of people liked Bill. A lot of people thought they knew him. But nobody really did. His whole life had been an act, and he had played whatever role it took to please people and get them to like or respect him.

The months of studying codependency and interacting with others had led to a series of revelations about himself: the anger that exploded from time to time, the hurt underneath, his need to control people, how others controlled him with only a raised eyebrow or slight change in tone of voice, his "for me or against me" perspective of people, his dogmatism in arguments because he "had to be right," his fear that he may be wrong, and the masks he wore as he played roles in his relationships.

In one meeting the leader described the "false self"—the person we try to be and the image of ourselves we try to project to others. The leader then asked, "What are some differences between your *false self* and your *real self*, the person who doesn't play games to block pain and win approval?"

Several people answered, but Bill sat still. He was usually a very active participant in the discussions, but this time he was strangely quiet. The leader noticed Bill's vacant expression and asked, "Bill, what are you thinking? Do you mind telling us?"

Bill continued to stare straight ahead into the oblivion of the far wall as he said slowly, "I just realized that I don't know who I am. I've played all these games to be successful, but . . . all that doesn't really matter." He paused. Then he said "I just want to be loved," and began to cry softly.

All of us have a God-given need to love and be loved.

All of us have a God-given need to love and be loved. Bonding is the earliest and most fundamental emotional developmental stage.[1] If a child experiences the affection, intimacy, and both emotional and physical nurturing of his parents, he has a firm foundation for a healthy identity. His need for defense mechanisms to block pain and gain approval is diminished, and he will be more likely to make progress toward successful independence. To the degree that these fundamental needs are not met, however, his development is blocked. When his God-given desire for love is unmet, he feels empty and his desire becomes a craving. Corresponding defense mechanisms are developed to limit the degree of hurt. The drive for success is often substituted for genuine love.

As we saw in the previous chapter, some of us experience neglect, or a lack of bonding. Others experience unhealthy bonds with dominating, smothering, or abusive parents. Many face a baffling combination of these extremes.

BURIED CRAVING

We want to be loved. We need to be loved. We try everything we can think of to experience love, but it is elusive. Something is wrong, and we assume it is *us*. It's like we are standing at a water fountain. We are thirsty and want to drink, but our arms won't work to push the button to get the water to come out. We see others come up, drink, and go away satisfied—or so it seems. We try again, and again, and again. We are angry . . . ashamed . . . confused . . . and alone.

Or some of us may feel as if we're standing at a huge banquet table full of delicious-looking food. Our stomachs rumble from hunger, but we've eaten food like this before and it was poisoned. We are afraid. Others eat and survive. But we can't . . . there's too much risk of being poisoned again.

Many passages of Scripture invite us to be satisfied by the love of God. For instance, Isaiah recorded:

> Ho! Every one who thirsts, come to the waters;
> And you who have no money come, buy and eat.
> Come, buy wine and milk
> Without money and without cost.
> Why do you spend money for what is not bread,
> And your wages for what does not satisfy?
> Listen carefully to Me, and eat what is good,
> And delight yourself in abundance.
> Incline your ear and come to Me.
> Listen, that you may live;
> And I will make an everlasting covenant with you,
> According to the faithful mercies shown to David (Isaiah 55:1–3).

We listen to pastors quote people like Augustine who experienced a deep quenching of his thirst for God: "Thou hast made us for Thyself, O God, and our hearts are restless until they find their rest in Thee."

> *. . .When we get a glimpse of reality,
> we feel ashamed that we can't seem to find what
> others have.*

Rest? Satisfaction? Intimacy? Sometimes we try to convince ourselves that we really are experiencing these things, and we tell others we feel so content. But it's a lie. We feel okay as long as we continue to fool ourselves. But when we get a glimpse of reality, we feel ashamed that we can't seem to find what others have. Again, something must be wrong with us!

Our unmet needs somehow imply that we aren't worthy of being loved. We've held our arms out and done all we know how to do, but we haven't felt hugged. That hurts even worse, so we decide never to hold our arms out again. We bury our craving for love.

> *. . .Some tangible gain is sought to
> replace the absence of love, the truly meaningful
> intangible.*

PROVING OURSELVES

When we don't experience love, we try to prove our value in some other way: success in business, sports, or clubs; prestige through promotions; power over other employees, family, and neighbors; acquiring money or things; finding pleasurable escapes or vacations; or making others happy by fixing their problems. In most of these, some tangible gain is sought to replace the absence of love, the truly meaningful intangible.

A counselor observed a lady's drive to attain success and promotions in her work. She asked the lady, "Why do you have to prove yourself?"

"I want to be somebody," she retorted. "I don't want to be worthless or mediocre." Later in the conversation, she reflected, "I have to get attention. When I don't get it, I feel like I don't even exist."

People are driven to prove themselves as they try to fill the hole left by unmet needs for love. "But wait," you may say, "Does that mean people who feel loved are unmotivated? Are they slobs? Is it better to stay driven and prove myself?"

People who have a relatively healthy identity, who can give and receive love, are usually highly motivated people. But they are motivated by entirely different standards. Their motivation comes more from *wanting to* succeed than *having to*. Their response to success (or failure) is not so black or white. They are not so threatened by failure or so prideful about success. If we become completely motivated by compulsion and guilt, we cannot conceive of another way to live.

NUMBING OUR WANTS

Some have given up trying to prove their worth, or become too frightened to try, so they numb both their pains and their wants. Alcohol and drugs are the most common numbing agents. Stimulants and depressants both change our experience of reality and block our hurt.

Constant busyness is another numbing agent. Some of us schedule so many things to do that we have very little time for reflection. This usually subconscious scheduling may be filled with many "good" things, but the goal is the same as alcohol or drugs: to numb the pain of an empty life.

Entertainment can deaden our sense of hurt as well. Movies, TV, video games, and similar pursuits are amusing diversions for a healthy person. But for many of us they have a different purpose: to help us escape from strained relationships and the festering accumulation of repressed painful emotions.

As we block the hurt, fear, and anger, we also suppress joy, love, and fun. It is the price we pay to keep from feeling emotions that threaten us.

Of course, some of us are so adept at numbing ourselves that we don't even need drugs, alcohol, busyness, or entertainment. We have repressed our feelings so completely for so long that we are almost emotional zombies. Our repression is not selective, however. As we block the hurt, fear, and anger, we also suppress joy, love, and fun. It is the price we pay to keep from feeling emotions that threaten us.

HATING OUR WANTS

We may try to substitute success and other things for love. We may bury our needs and numb our desires. But when we do become aware of these desires for love, intimacy, warmth, and acceptance, we are likely to sense a surge of hatred. We hate the fact that we have needs.

. . .*Our wants show us how empty we really are.*

Why such a violent response? Because our wants show us how empty we really are. Our pain rises to the surface, stark and intense. And a common interpretation of that feeling is, *I am worse than unloved. I am unlovable.* We hate those who reject us. We hate ourselves for being so worthless. And we hate our wants because they scream out that we are worthless.

Beth had tried everything she could think of to get people to care about her. She tried being a "good little girl," and then a rebel in a tough gang. She tried sex and booze. She became a Christian and adopted all the "right rules" of the faith. At that point her pastor pointed to her as the ultimate testimony of a changed life. Yet while there *were* changes, a thick layer of *something* still kept God's love and others' care from penetrating through to the core of her life.

She finally realized she couldn't play the game any longer. She thought, *I'm a good Christian on the outside, but I want to be loved so much. Sometimes I realize how empty I am . . . and how much I want to feel loved. It hurts so badly I can't stand it! I hate my wants, and I hate myself for wanting.*

The Bible has much to say of God's love and grace. It describes intimate relationships possible within the church. God's love is promised to be right there for us, both through Himself and His people. So what's the problem?

Paradoxically, those who crave love prevent themselves from experiencing it. They search in the wrong places because they don't know what real love looks like. They settle for substitutes. Their paralyzed arms don't allow them to drink at the fountain even though they see others enjoying the water. Their fear of the banquet food prevents them from eating so they will not be poisoned again.

A successful businessman had been in counseling for several months. Walt realized that his drive to attain wealth and prestige had actually been an attempt to replace the love he really wanted. He recalled that while his father had provided for the family financially, he had rarely shown love in any verbal or physical way. His father hadn't been cruel; he had been aloof.

Walt reflected on his own accomplishments and the emptiness in his life. He said, "I would give every dollar I've earned, every promotion I've gotten, every vacation I've enjoyed . . . I'd give everything I've got to be loved by my dad . . . but it won't happen. Sometimes I feel so lonely and empty, though none of my family and nobody at the office would believe that. Sometimes I want to kill him . . . and then I feel so ashamed for thinking something so terrible."

The craving for love is usually coupled with another opposite, reactive emotion: *fear*. We are afraid we won't receive the love we crave.

We may be afraid that we aren't worthy of being loved. We may fear that if we experience love, it won't be enough to satisfy us and fill our emptiness. We may fear that if we pursue love, we will be hurt more than ever. Though we may intensely crave to be loved, our fear stands in the way.

The next chapter will address several of these specific fears and how they prevent us from experiencing the love we so desperately crave.

REFLECTION/DISCUSSION

1. What are some differences between "wanting" and "craving"?

2. Do you think it is normal to crave love? Why or why not?

3. What is your definition of love?

4. How have you misunderstood love in the past?

5. Review this chapter and determine how you may have used each of the following defenses to keep from feeling the hurt and emptiness of not loving and being loved.

    Buried Craving

    Proving Yourself

    Numbing Your Wants

6. What is the most delightful relationship you have ever experienced? What made that relationship so special?

7.   Paraphrase the following passages:

Romans 5:8

1 John 3:1

Romans 8:38–39

Lamentations 3:19–24

8.   How can you experience more of God's love?

[1] For an explanation of bonding and other developmental stages, see *Your Parents and You*, Robert S. McGee, Jim Craddock, and Pat Springle. (Houston and Dallas, TX: Rapha Publishing/Word, Inc., 1990),pp. 29–60.

5

◆

Fear

—*Robert S. McGee*

A MAN WHO HAD BEEN IN A SUPPORT GROUP for two years told me, "In the last couple of months, I have been far more aware of my fears than ever before. In the past, when somebody controlled me or rejected me, or I failed, or *whatever* happened, I felt some amorphous sense of tension inside me that I never even tried to identify. I thought it was just a normal part of life. When big confrontations took place, I would be so consumed with them that I couldn't sleep. I had a knot in my stomach. I would think about the people involved for hours and hours, analyzing everything that had happened—and everything that could possibly happen!

"Oh, I've known I had fears for a long time, but until recently I didn't realize how deeply and completely I was controlled by them. A few weeks ago someone said something sarcastic to me about my work. I felt the old tension level rise, but then I realized, *I am afraid.* Those words sounded like a new language to me: strange . . . awkward . . . but accurate. I sat and thought for a few minutes. It was so strange because I realized how many zillions of times I had felt that way and not been able to identify the feeling as fear."

"What were you afraid of?" I asked.

"That's a good question. I realized that it was more than the fear of rejection. I was afraid that I would be a nobody. That's it. A nobody. If my work was attacked, my identity as a 'good employee' was threatened, and if I didn't have that identity . . . well, I wasn't sure who I would be. I was afraid of being a zero . . . a nobody . . . nothing. Even to talk about it now seems strange. Going from not being able to identify a feeling I've had so many times to identifying it and seeing its fundamental threat to my life is pretty overwhelming."

He paused for a minute. "Can I tell you something really weird? I'm kind of excited about all this," he said sheepishly. "I think I'm making progress!"

The "fog of war" is the confusing, chaotic environment of smoke, noise, bullets, and bombs where men have great difficulty picking out and responding to individual elements of the battle. This man had begun to see through the "fog of fear," that bewildering conglomeration of fear, hurt, anger, repressed emotions from the past, the demand for an instant response, and the pressure to be right.

When our deepest needs for "irrational love" (to use Burton White's term) are unmet, a void is created and a craving for love develops. We fear that our needs won't be met, that someone we trust will hurt us—again. Some of us are only too aware of our fears. Others are unable to identify the emotion of fear amid the confusing and threatening morass of other painful emotions.

Broadly speaking, women tend to be more "in touch" with hurt and fear while men identify with anger. Much of our behavior is in response to our cultural mores. Anger is a "man's emotion," perceived as macho. Hurt and fear are for wimps—or women. It is more socially acceptable for women to confess to hurt and fear because they are more often perceived as needy than overtly powerful. Anger is too brutish and coarse for women.

Yet men do experience hurt and fear, and women get angry. In fact, the healing process of men can often be measured by their ability to come to grips with the hurt and fear beneath their anger. And while more women have the willingness to admit anger than men do to admit hurt and fear, that anger may be the most threatening emotion they have. It reminds them of being abused. They may believe that feeling anger will make them lose control, and consequently be less of a woman.

We can be afraid of all kinds of things that seem to threaten us—sometimes even the things we want most. Some of our reactions may be very mild, or we may become shackled by overwhelming fear and even experience panic attacks. Let's examine a few of the most common fears.

COMMON FEARS

FEAR OF: REJECTION
           INTIMACY
           FAILURE
           SUCCESS
           BEING CREATIVE
           BEING KNOWN
           NOT BEING KNOWN
           BEING HURT AGAIN
           BETRAYING THE FAMILY
           NOT BEING SOMEBODY

FEAR OF REJECTION

Since the most fundamental need is to be loved, this is the most fundamental fear. Almost all other fears have their roots in this one. Fear of rejection is fueled by previous beatings, sarcasm, comparison, neglect, verbal condemnation for minor errors, not being trusted, and a host of other experiences. We may have been abused, abandoned, or smothered, and we don't want to experience those things any longer. Our defenses are up, and every event or person that threatens our fragile coping system receives a defensive response because we are afraid of potential rejection.

Many of us cannot even believe that God really loves us. We may sing praises at church. We may put on a happy smile for other

Christians so we look like model believers. But secretly, we're afraid that God's forgiveness doesn't extend quite far enough to cover the things we've done. We wonder if He really loves us. We're afraid that we will do something—if we haven't already done so—that will cause us to lose our salvation.

FEAR OF INTIMACY

When other people express love and appreciation—the very things we crave—many of us push them away. We may be afraid that we will be hurt again. We will trust and love . . . and then be dropped.

"I can't get close to anybody. It hurts too much," Lou Ann told me. "I feel so mixed up. The very thing I want is the thing I am so afraid of."

FEAR OF FAILURE

For many of us, failure threatens our sense of identity by implying that we are unworthy people. Frank related, "I remember hearing my Dad say, 'Nothing you do is good enough.' And I remember my sister trying so hard to be best in school and in the band. She did really well, but she too would express, 'Nothing I do is good enough.' Then she quit—she quit trying." Frank reflected for a few minutes, "I feel that way, too. I've done really well at some things and really badly at others, but even when I do well, all I see are the errors. I feel bad when I fail, but I feel bad when I succeed too, because nothing I do is good enough."

FEAR OF SUCCESS

We see others do well, and we get jealous. We crave the attention they receive, but we also fear that if we succeed and get recognition that it won't be enough. Then we'll be really empty because hope for fulfillment will be lost.

"I find some way to sabotage the things I do," Sue explained. "I do well up to a point, but I never go past that point. I never risk trying a solo or asking to write the final proposal on a job at work. I'm afraid I'll blow it . . . but I'm also afraid I wouldn't be able to handle it if I did well. I feel so confused!"

FEAR OF BEING CREATIVE

Some of us are not encouraged to be creative as children. We may have been neglected, controlled, or condemned when we tried something new.

"I loved to draw so much," Ken said in regard to his childhood desires. "But my dad would walk in and make some sarcastic comment about every drawing I did. He laughed about his witty observations, and I laughed with him. But I stopped drawing. His comments were funny, but they made me feel like a failure. I wanted him to love me, not make fun of me."

"How has that affected you as an adult?" I asked.

"Well, I don't try too many creative projects either at work or at home. I have this nagging sense of guilt when I try something, so it's easier to not try at all. But then I feel angry because I'm being controlled. I know I can do some creative things, but I feel trapped."

FEAR OF BEING KNOWN

*E*veryone has defense mechanisms and hide themselves to some degree, but some of us are terrified by people knowing what we are like.

Everyone has defense mechanisms and hide themselves to some degree, but some of us are terrified by people knowing what we are like. Our sins and the sins of our families have to be kept secret, or else. This fear is reflected in statements such as:

- "If he really knew what I'm like, he'd leave me."

- "If they understood how I think and feel, they'd never be my friends."

- "If they knew all about me, they'd never hire me."

- "I'll let people know me to a point, but when they try to get past that point I shut them out."

Sir Arthur Conan Doyle, the author of the Sherlock Holmes series, played a practical joke on a dozen friends. He sent each of them a telegram reading only, "Flee at once. All is discovered." The next day, all twelve had left the country!

FEAR OF NOT BEING KNOWN

At the opposite extreme from those who are afraid to let themselves be known are those who are afraid no one will know them. So they "spill their guts," hoping that transparency and intimacy will draw people close. Sharing secrets may produce absorbing friendships, but these bonds are usually broken brutally whenever a trust is betrayed.

Another reason to "tell all" is, paradoxically, to keep people away. "I have a compulsion to tell people everything about myself," Rhonda said. "If I tell them a lot, then they are responsible for the friendship. I almost push them to leave by telling them so much trash about myself."

Another lady quietly explained why she feared not being known: "When I grew up, my parents spent very little time with me, and when Christmas or my birthday came around, they always gave me things I didn't want. They weren't bad things, but they just weren't what I wanted. Mom and Dad never got to know me: what I like, what I'm interested in, the styles I preferred. They just gave me what they thought I'd like. I wanted them to know me, to understand me. The presents symbolized the fact that they didn't. I lived in their house, but they didn't know me at all."

FEAR OF BEING HURT AGAIN

Some of us have been so deeply wounded that we now live behind a fortress of defense mechanisms, afraid of being hurt again. Almost every interaction is seen as a threat. We are always on guard, always keeping people away, yet always craving intimacy. The possibility of receiving intimacy, however, is overshadowed by the risk of more pain.

This double bind is personified in a woman who was quite fragile emotionally. She ingratiated herself to others, desperately wanting their affirmation and respect. Whenever someone responded positively to her, she subconsciously pushed them away by finding fault in them, blaming them for the least offense (or perceived offense), being late, or failing to complete a task which the other person had counted on. Her behavior reflected the same message as a confused child who screamed, "I need you. Go away!"

FEAR OF BETRAYING THE FAMILY

People from dysfunctional families tend to feel tremendous responsibility to protect other family members, even those who have committed heinous abuses.

One major factor that hinders a person's emotional and spiritual recovery is the fear of betraying family secrets. People from dysfunctional families tend to feel tremendous responsibility to protect other family members, even those who have committed heinous abuses. In fact, the more abusive the family members, the more blind loyalty a person may have toward them.

The reality of betraying the family usually stems from a combination of powerful factors:

Actual threats—Abusive family members may threaten physical or emotional reprisals—either verbal or nonverbal. The abused person has previously experienced very painful consequences when "stepping out of line" for the smallest offense, so threats have a powerful effect to control him.

Lack of objectivity—To some, it is shocking that so many abused people believe the abuser loves them. It's not uncommon to hear, "She couldn't help it. I deserved to be hit like that because I'm such a bad person. She really loves me. I'm sure of that!"

Lack of choice—Coupled with the lack of objectivity is the absence of viable options for an abused person. As a child dominated by his parents, he simply has nowhere else to turn. This hopeless perception is internalized over the years. Even as an adult living far from the abusers, he may not be able to identify the differences between healthy and abusive relationships. It seems normal to gravitate toward familiar, abusive relationships, and the emotional problems continue.

Those from relatively healthy families cannot imagine the tremendous, oppressive sense of guilt an abused person experiences when he begins to even *think* about telling another person the truth about his family. It takes great courage to risk betraying the family secret, but the healing process often turns on this single issue.

FEAR OF NOT BEING SOMEBODY

We crave a sense of identity, of place, of being. And we fear that we may be nobodies. Ironically, this very fear leads many of us to become puppets, doing whatever it takes to please others. Instead of having an internal sense of value that comes with true identity, we try to manufacture one based on our performance and the approval of others. We are easily controlled, and try to control others in turn. We establish few limits in decision-making and poor boundaries in relationships.

Instead of having the security of feeling loved for who we are, our choices boil down to either giving in to our fear or reacting against it. A friend told me, "My fear of being a nobody steals my freedom to be myself and make my own choices. The other day someone at work asked me to go to lunch. He asked, 'Where do you want to go?' and I told him, 'I'd like a hamburger.' He said, 'Aw, you always eat hamburgers. You ought to have a pizza!' I felt the tension and fear levels rise in me. I only seemed to have two choices: to give in, or to react and insist, 'Heck, no! I'm not going to eat a pizza! I'm going to eat a hamburger!' Either way, giving in or reacting, I felt like a nobody."

We seldom recognize our fears because we are so steeped in them, yet they are intensely threatening to us because we know of no other ways to cope with life.

We seldom recognize our fears because we are so steeped in them, yet they are intensely threatening to us because we know of no other ways to cope with life. Unbridled fears can color every thought, every action, and every relationship. They can make us aggressive (bragging, sarcastic, driven) or passive (withdrawn, depressed, acquiescent).

The reason our fears are so powerfully negative and consuming is because they are wedded to the helplessness and hopelessness of shame, which is the topic of the next chapter.

REFLECTION/DISCUSSION

1. What are some reasons for the difficulty in detecting your fears?

2. How, then, can you know what you fear?

3. Rate the degree to which each of the following fears is present in your life, and then describe how the significant ones (mid-scale and up) affect your relationships, decisions, goals, and desires.

Fear of:	1 Severe	2 Much	3 Somewhat	4 Little	5 None
Rejection	❏	❏	❏	❏	❏
Intimacy	❏	❏	❏	❏	❏
Failure	❏	❏	❏	❏	❏
Success	❏	❏	❏	❏	❏
Being Creative	❏	❏	❏	❏	❏
Being Known	❏	❏	❏	❏	❏
Not Being Known	❏	❏	❏	❏	❏
Being Hurt Again	❏	❏	❏	❏	❏
Betraying the Family	❏	❏	❏	❏	❏
Not Being Somebody	❏	❏	❏	❏	❏

4. Fear of betraying the family is a common, paralyzing fear. Why do you think this fear is so threatening?

5. How can a progressive understanding of Christ's forgiveness, love, and acceptance help to calm fears?

6

◆

Shame

—Robert S. McGee

Many of our fears can be traced to a common source—an interior sense of shame. The *fear* of being a nobody usually stems from the *sense* of being a nobody. Feelings of helplessness and hopelessness generally result when a child internalizes the deficiency of love and security in the home concluding, *Something's wrong with me! I must be a bad person. I am unlovable.*

Most psychologists differentiate between guilt and shame. Guilt is the realization that your behavior is in error. It focuses on actions—what you did. Shame is internalized, unforgiven guilt or ungrieved wounds. Shame focuses on identity—who you are.

Many of us feel unworthy of anyone's attention and affection. Janice related, "Sometimes I feel lonely, and I don't think anybody really wants to get to know me. Then I wish somebody would pursue me . . . would want to be my friend. But even that desire is cut short because I'm afraid if anybody really gets to know me, they would see that I really am unworthy of their friendship. . . . I couldn't stand that."

Several factors can compound and complicate our sense of shame: painful parental relationships; past events that are so devastating that they color our present and future; the inability to stop a bad habit; our appearance; and perpetuating unhealthy relationships.

SOURCES OF SHAME

PAINFUL PARENTAL RELATIONSHIPS

PAST EVENTS SO BAD . . .

BAD HABITS

APPEARANCE

UNHEALTHY ATTACHMENTS

PAINFUL PARENTAL RELATIONSHIPS

Our identity is shaped largely by the reflections our parents communicate to us. If those mirrors reflect love and strength, we will probably develop a healthy sense of who we are. To the degree that the mirrors reflect that we are unlovable or that our value is based on our ability to please them, then our identity will be distorted.

We feel unloved, insecure, frightened, and driven. We believe we can never do enough to please others so that they will accept us—or give us the love we crave. We become puppets, doing whatever others want us to do, or islands, avoiding meaningful interaction to escape any further rejection.

PAST EVENTS SO BAD . . .

Many of us are haunted by the past. The events themselves may have been either significant or relatively minor, but we placed monumental importance on them. Sexual sins, lying, cheating, back-stabbing, acts of greed or dispassion, vandalism, or stealing come to mind over and over again like the methodical thud of a sledge hammer. No less devastating is the perceived negative importance of relatively minor offenses.

One lady grew up in a very strict, religious home. On her 16th birthday, she and a friend drank a beer—only one—but she felt that she had transgressed a major commandment of God. Though she tried the penance of "feeling bad enough, long enough," her overwhelming sense of unforgiveness turned to shame. (Actually, this lady had already developed a deep and pervasive sense of shame, but she points to this particular event rather than the rigidity and harshness of her home environment as the cause of it.

Another person described the shamefulness he felt because he had trusted an unscrupulous man in a financial arrangement. "I put up some money—quite a lot of money—because I felt sure this guy was on the level. Later, I had lost it all, and he wouldn't do anything about it. I feel like such a jackass for trusting him. Every time I pay a bill it reminds me how much money I wasted and how stupid I was to trust him."

BAD HABITS

"I want to stop drinking. I've tried—really tried, but I can't!"

"I . . . I don't know how to stop, you know, looking at those magazines and movies. I know it's wrong. I've confessed it a thousand times, but. . . ."

"Every time I yell at my children, I hate myself so much! I would do anything to stop! It's so bad for them. They're afraid of me. I can't stand it. I treat them just like Dad treated me. I hated the way he treated me, but I do the very same thing to my children!"

"My house is a pigpen. I want it to be clean and nice for my family, but I just can't seem to get around to it. Sometimes I start, but now it is such a big job. . . ."

Bad habits—or rather the inability to conquer them—produce and perpetuate shame in our lives. When food, sex, alcohol, drugs, anger, or continued irresponsibility in any area of life controls us, our confidence is sapped. We feel hopeless and try to hide.

APPEARANCE

Fat. Bald. Skinny legs. Big rear. Out-of-style clothes. Pock-marked face. A figure like a gourd. Stringy hair. Ski ramp nose. Rotten smile. The list of derogative physical attributes is almost endless—and almost endlessly painful.

In the age of beautiful people on television and magazines, appearance has taken on an almost all-encompassing importance. Fifty years ago, we may have compared ourselves (and been compared) to others in our towns or neighborhoods. Now the standard is raised. We compare ourselves to airbrushed pictures of the most gorgeous models in the world. Is it any wonder we don't measure up when we look in the mirror?

Many of us try desperately to look as good as we possibly can, and our thoughts are consumed by our flaws and the opportunity to overcome those flaws. Others of us have given up. We may despise the way we look, but we don't do anything to make ourselves look presentable and reasonably attractive. The healthy balance of thankfulness, self-acceptance, and moderate expenditure of time and money escapes us.

One woman told me that she spends almost every waking hour worrying about her hair, clothes, weight, complexion, nails, and other aspects of her appearance. Many men are just as preoccupied, though usually not as obvious about it. They evaluate their "pecs," scrutinize and despair over every hair dropped in the sink, and compare clothes and shapes as much as women do.

Though we may crave love, many of us are drawn to unloving people like magnets. . . perhaps we feel that we don't deserve better, lack objectivity, need to be needed, or need to control and be controlled.

UNHEALTHY ATTACHMENTS

Another factor which perpetuates shame in our lives is the attachment to people who continue to inflict pain and withhold affirmation. Though we may crave love, many of us are drawn to unloving people like magnets. We may be attracted to them because that's what we've seen other family members do. Or perhaps we feel that we don't deserve better, lack objectivity, need to be needed, or need to control and be controlled.

One man told how he seemed to gravitate to employers who dominated him. "I'm so afraid at work," he told me. "My boss is demanding and manipulative. I thought I would enjoy it here, but I can't take it much longer."

As we talked, he described other jobs he had held, each with bosses who were overbearing in some way. He also told me about his mother's demanding, controlling manner. After a while, he saw a connection between his mother's actions and attitudes, and his employer's. "But why would I look for people to treat me like my mother has?" he asked.

Rachel told me about her absorbing, codependent relationships. "I want to help people . . . you know, be a servant to them. And they need somebody to help them so much. I can't just let them suffer without helping them." As Rachel began to see the unhealthy attachments involved in these relationships, she also began to see some new choices. She could continue the familiar, strangely comfortable but painful patterns of rescuing and being rescued, or she could learn to set limits and become more independent.

FALSE HUMILITY AND FALSE PRIDE

Without a secure sense of identity, we often try to cover and compensate for our needs and hurts with false humility and false pride. False humility is putting ourselves down publicly, calling attention to our "nothingness" in an attempt to elicit attention and pity from others. When we succeed, we may say, "Oh, it wasn't really very good," hoping others will say, "Sure it was good. In fact, it was great!" And when we fail, we may say, "I'm such a zero. I can't ever do anything right," hoping others will give reassurance and praise.

False pride is another response to shame and the fear of being a nobody. Insecurity leads some of us to brag about our accomplishments, boasting that the job couldn't be done without us, calling attention to our indispensable contribution. Failure is swept under the carpet in denial while others are blamed.

We also have many other ways we try to cover and compensate for our shame. These surface most clearly in our responses to success and failure.

RESPONDING TO SUCCESS

People who experience oppressive shame respond to success and failure in fairly predictable ways—but always in extremes. When we succeed:

We feel excessively proud. We live for success and appreciation, so when it comes, we may be quite grandiose about our accomplishments. We tend to be black-and-white, seeing people and events as all bad or all good, so our successes may be described as "the best," "the most," or "the greatest." If others had a role in the success, we may downplay their contributions because we don't want to share our glory with anyone else.

We discount it. "Oh, it wasn't any big deal. Anybody could have done it—and probably a lot better, too." Unable to cope with the success we long for, some of us find ways to discount it.

We deny it. Some of us are so afraid of success that we deny it altogether. "No, it was really bad. People are just trying to be nice to me by telling me it was good, but I know the truth. It was a flop."

We pass it. "Thanks, but Jane was the one who really made the campaign a success. It would never have worked without her. I really didn't do that much." We may feel so uncomfortable in the spotlight of attention that we try to pass it to someone—anyone—else.

We may also pass it to God. I congratulated a high school student for giving a good speech. Her response was very pious. "It wasn't me. It was God."

That's funny, I thought to myself, *I sure thought I saw her lips moving.*

In our relationships with God, He has a role and so do we. Paul reminded the Corinthian believers that they were "working together with Him" (2 Cor. 6:1). We need to avoid self-righteousness at one extreme, but we also need to avoid denial and passivity on the other.

We analyze it. Many of us "live in our heads" by analyzing everything we say and do as well as everything others say and do toward us. When we succeed, we may relive the experience over and over, enjoying the rush of affirmation. Or we may meticulously pick apart even the most glowing success, condemning our performance and ourselves.

RESPONDING TO FAILURE

We go to the other extreme in our responses to failure:

We condemn ourselves. If excessive pride is our response to success, then self-condemnation is our response to failure, or even perceived failure.

"I did it again. I knew I would. I'm nothing but a lousy...." Probably all of us have names we call ourselves, but people shackled by worthlessness and self-hatred give themselves exceptionally vile names. I asked a young man what names he calls himself when he fails. He looked shocked, then frightened. "I don't think I want to tell you," he said very slowly. "They're not the kind of things you hear in Sunday School." Indeed, they are not.

We discount it. Some of us can't stand the reality of failure, so we discount it. "It's not that bad. Aw, it's not going to hurt anybody. It's no big deal anyway."

We deny it. Some of us deny failure completely, pushing it out of our minds and going on to some other task. We may vacillate between the twin evils of self-condemnation and denial, robbing ourselves of constructive objectivity and helpful input from others.

We pass it. "It's not my fault!" she blurted out. "I did all I could do with him, but my husband, Dan, didn't do anything to help." Sara's son was having behavior problems at school. The teacher and the principal had called Sara and her husband in for a consultation, but Sara couldn't accept any responsibility for her son's problems at all. She could only blame her husband.

We analyze it. We may relive successes to enjoy them again, but most analytical people focus far more on their *failures*. It is the negative experiences that are relived over and over, as the person condemns himself for every conceivable wrong, wishing he had done something different, and vowing to do it some other way next time.

TRYING TO DREAM AWAY THE SHAME

Shame-filled people have learned that painful emotions are bad and out of control, so they usually put tight clamps on them. They repress anger, hurt, and fear, but sooner or later these volcanic feelings erupt in explosions of self-pity and pain. Thinking without feeling gives way to feeling without thinking. When emotions are "stuffed" over a prolonged period, we may become emotionally numb or depressed.

All of us daydream, but deeply wounded people often retreat into a fantasy world of wonderful things that make them feel secure, strong, and happy—or horrible things which they dread happening to them and their loved ones. Often they vacillate between these two extremes quite readily.

Lou told me her mind wanders a lot. She said, "I like to think about being married to a handsome, loving man. We'd have beautiful children, and we'd go on vacations to places like Jamaica. I spend lots of time thinking about being with him on an island, the two of us in love. But then, out of nowhere, I imagine him being eaten by a shark or killed by a hurricane. I see myself, crying and alone again."

Fantasies are a convenient way to escape the gnawing pains of shame, but the safe haven of daydreams often becomes the nightmare of imagined, almost tangible, fear, hurt, and anger.

Dealing with shame is often a painfully slow process that requires setting limits, saying no, learning to make our own decisions, and peeling off layers of defense mechanisms. When we begin to see the deeper causes and effects of shame, our identity is changed, and we begin to believe that we have value apart from our performance and the approval of others. After we confront our hidden shame, every aspect of our lives will grow and change.

EXPOSING SHAME WITHOUT REGRET

Shame has the power to crush and destroy because our feelings of worthlessness are compounded by the fear of exposure. We live with the dread that people will find out that we are deficient, incompetent, and undesirable. If we were sure these threatening traits could remain hidden, we would feel safe. We can't help thinking, *What if my wife* (or parent, or husband, or child, or friend, or minister, or . . .) *finds out what a bad person I really am?*

We feel vulnerable, so we hide. We develop elaborate defense mechanisms to keep others (and ourselves?) from knowing how utterly despicable we are. When Adam and Eve sinned in the Garden, they felt shame and immediately covered their nakedness and tried to hide from God.

We hide in different ways: not being willing to admit when we are wrong, being driven to succeed, pleasing people at all costs, never taking risks, taking huge risks, being tough, and having no opinions at all, to name a few. In all these, we live behind facades. We develop a false self because we don't want our true (undesirable, worthless, despicable) self to be exposed.

*O*ne *major step to take toward overcoming shame is the willingness to discuss the "family secret" with a friend or counselor.*

One major step to take toward overcoming shame is the willingness to discuss the "family secret" with a friend or counselor. A measure of trust and courage is required to take that risk, but talking about our families often brings the first big results toward healing. Another major step (or series of steps) is the exposing of our personal secrets: our deepest fears, hurts, longings, and angers. This exposure is not just a matter of talking about these issues and emotions, but *experiencing* them; not analyzing them, but living them. We cannot fully grieve a sterile analysis of previous losses. We must release what we have kept hidden for so long.

We fear exposure for good reason: in the past we have been laughed at, ridiculed, neglected and abused when our faults have been exposed. but the Gospel has the power to heal when we stop covering up and hiding. Before a loving, gracious, compassionate God, we are fully exposed. The writer to the Hebrews wrote:

> The word of God is living and active and sharper than any two-edged sword, and piercing as far as the division of soul and spirit, of both joints and marrow, and able to judge the thoughts and intentions of the heart.
> And there is no creature hidden from His sight, but all things are open and laid bare to the eyes of Him with whom we have to do (Hebrews 4:12–13).

THOUGH WE ARE EXPOSED, WE NEED NOT BE RIDICULED.
THOUGH WE ARE EXPOSED, WE NEED NOT BE LAUGHED AT.
THOUGH WE ARE EXPOSED, WE NEED NOT BE NEGLECTED.
THOUGH WE ARE EXPOSED, WE NEED NOT BE ABUSED.

We are exposed, and we are deeply loved. Isn't that the healing power of the Gospel? Isn't that what makes Jesus Christ the *Good Shepherd*? Isn't that what draws us to the Father's kindness, gentleness, and strong love . . . that encourages us to respond "Abba [which means Daddy] Father"? (See Romans 8:15.)

Hiding is a reasonable and understandable defense mechanism. But hiding is unnecessary with God. We are exposed, but He makes us feel safe, strong, and loved.

REFLECTION/DISCUSSION

1. The square on the following page represents your life. Shade the amount you are ashamed of:

Your Life

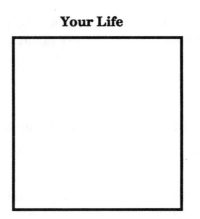

2. Describe how each of following has contributed to your sense of shame.

   • Painful Parental Relationships

   • Past Events So Bad . . .

   • Bad Habits

   • Appearance

   • Unhealthy Attachments

   In what ways are these *causes* of shame, and in what ways are they *results* of shame?

3. What are some characteristics of false humility? Of false pride?

4. How do you respond to success and failure? How do those responses reflect your sense of shame?

5. Do you daydream quite a bit? Describe your last daydream. What might your daydreams say about you?

6. What is the difference between shame and remorse for our sins?

7. Forgiveness and a sense of identity are crucial in overcoming shame. Paraphrase these passages:

   • Colossians 1:12–14

   • Colossians 2:13–14

   • 1 Peter 2:9–10

8. Why is exposure—or the fear of exposure—a component of shame?

9. Describe your fear of exposure. (How does it affect you? What are your methods of hiding? How much of yourself have you exposed so far in the healing process? What's the next step for you?)

10. How do you feel about the truth that you are fully exposed to the Lord and fully loved by Him?

7

◆

Bitterness

—Pat Springle

Hatred is intense, unresolved anger. Bitterness is hatred that has been harbored and has festered. Over weeks, months, and years, anger from unforgiven wounds and injustices simmers in its own venom, increasing until it consumes the angry person.

Christians speak often of forgiveness and love; but ironically, they sometimes have a difficult time applying those biblical truths to their own anger and hatred. In too many Sunday School classes and other church groups, well-meaning leaders condemn all feelings of anger as sin. They imply that only "bad Christians" feel anger. Few Christians can stand the threat of being labeled—as "bad"; their identities are too wrapped up in being "good." So they practice denial, trying to convince themselves that their anger and hatred isn't really anger and hatred at all. "I'm just *frustrated*," they claim. Meanwhile, the repression continues and the anger builds. They explode from time to time and then feel ashamed of themselves, doing penance by feeling bad enough, long enough to pay for the terrible sin of exploding in anger. But they fail to find a true biblical solution, one that encompasses the causes of their emotions and differentiates between feeling angry and taking revenge. As a result, they fail to begin the process of healing that can help them actually experience Paul's admonishment to the believers at Ephesus: "Be angry, and yet do not sin; do not let the sun go down on your anger, and do not give the devil an opportunity" (Ephesians 4:26-27).

Once, a friend of mine accidentally cut his hand with a knife. Instead of accepting the compassion and help of those around him, he became tense and angry toward everyone. While motioning violently with his other hand, he glared at them and yelled, "Get back! Get away from me!" Later, he asked me, "Why would getting hurt produce such violence? There must be a lot of anger buried somewhere in me. In fact, I guess you could call it rage. I was really out of control."

It's natural for people to protect themselves against being hurt. Similarly, anger about being hurt is a natural, reflexive response, a defense reaction that may also be coupled with self-imposed isolation. When this response occurs, angry persons push others away, telling even friends and loved ones to "Get back!" Then the love and compassion they genuinely crave are overridden by defense mechanisms they believe will keep them from being hurt. As a result, they remain isolated and unconsoled, even when they need love most, and their anger festers into bitterness.

Some people remind us of ourselves. We may project our problems onto them, and we may even hate them for their similarities to us. Other people remind us of those who have hurt us deeply. In our minds, we transfer the characteristics of the hurtful person to the new person. For instance, if someone reminds me of my first employer, my instinctive response is to feel the same toward him as I did toward that employer.

In some families, expressing anger at parents or siblings brings quick condemnation. Members of those families learn to focus their anger on themselves instead of their parents or siblings.

HATING OURSELVES

Sometimes people feel hatred toward themselves. In some families, expressing anger at parents or siblings brings quick condemnation. Members of those families learn to focus their anger on themselves instead of their parents or siblings. The results are damaging to one's self-image.

Recently I led a group on the subject of anger and asked, "What kind of names do you call yourself?"

"Stupid," one gentleman said. A lady said she called herself "fat moron," though she was very attractive and obviously bright. Other responses were "dumb nerd," "jerk," and "scumball." When one person said, "I really can't tell this group. It's a little too crude," lots of other people nodded and laughed nervously.

I asked, "Do any of you call yourselves names like, 'smart,' 'beautiful,' 'handsome,' 'loved,' 'valuable,' or anything like that?"

A short, bald man in the back said, "Yeah." He paused and then added, "But I don't believe it!"

Everybody laughed again.

"If you heard a person calling someone else the names you call yourself, what conclusions would you come to? How would that person seem to feel about the other?"

Several people looked reflective; then a lady said, "I'd say the first one hates the other—*really hates* that person."

Many people call themselves degrading, derogatory names as punishment for the slightest mistakes. They take revenge on themselves by attacking or blaming themselves, or by withholding something they need. This condemnation often arises from implicit conclusions they drew long ago that they are bad, shameful people, unworthy of love, and fully deserving of all the pain they can inflict upon themselves . . . and probably much more. This continual condemnation can easily evolve into bitterness.

HATING OTHERS

Feelings of hurt and anger toward others often remain locked away due to blind loyalty, refusal to betray the "family secret," expected reprisals, or fear of the power these emotions would have if they were expressed.

As angry, hurting persons experience healing, they become increasingly objective about themselves and their families. They begin to feel the emotions they have repressed so long. They risk being honest (if only a little bit!) with those who help them feel safe, and the healing process continues.

Typically, people in denial protect and defend those who have hurt them. One woman who had been physically abused by her father and brother said, "I love them, and I know they love me. They just didn't know how to express it."

"*I*'d like to kill both of them for what they did to me!"

As she continued going to a group and listening to others, she began to see what love really is . . . and what it isn't. For several weeks, she sat in the group, quiet and confused. As realization slowly dawned on her, she entered a state of shock. "I can't believe it. I just can't believe it," she said over and over. A couple of months later, the group's nurturing environment had provided enough safety and strength for her repressed hatred to surface. One night she exploded. "I'd like to kill both of them for what they did to me!" she cried. As soon as she said it, she was overwhelmed with shame for having expressed what she truly felt. She then returned to emotional hiding. It took three more months before she could talk openly again in the group about her feelings toward her father and brother.

This woman's response was typical of those who finally come to grips with injustice that has been inflicted on them. A common sequence of responses is denial, initial realization, shock, explosions, shame, then more progress. After a while, people in this process cease to be surprised when more repressed hurt and anger are uncovered. "I'm not that surprised anymore," a friend admitted. "I used to be shocked every time I saw more of it, but I guess I'm more comfortable with the reality of the *depth* of my wounds. I don't expect quick cures like I did at first. We talk about 'the process,' and that's exactly what it is, a process of feeling and forgiving."

In the early stages of the healing process, most people become aware of the damage inflicted on them primarily by one or two people—for instance, a parent who was sexually abusive or who smothered the child with control. As the healing process continues, however, more intense anger may be revealed toward another person in the family, typically the other parent, who failed to protect the child from harm.

Describing her verbally abusive, controlling mother, Alicia said, "I couldn't even pick out which clothes to wear to school. Mother told me what to wear, who to spend time with, and even what to say to them. Every day she quizzed me about each conversation I'd had, and if I hadn't guessed what she wanted me to say, boy, she let me have it! I didn't have a life of my own."

"Tell me about your dad," I said.

"Oh, Dad was great. He never did all that kind of stuff to me. He spent most of his time in the den reading. He couldn't stand her, either!" she laughed.

"Did he ever stop your mother from controlling or criticizing you?"

"Well . . . no, not really. Sometimes he'd hear me crying in my room and come to tell me he understood. I appreciated that."

Alicia had trouble being objective about her mother because she believed her mother's control was the same as love. Slowly, however, she realized that love is not manipulative, smothering, and condemning. That's when Alicia started making real progress. Much later, however, as she grieved and learned to forgive her mother, Alicia's focus shifted to her father.

"All these years I felt so positive about my dad. I guess that's because he was nicer to me than Mother was. But now I realize that he could have done *a lot more* than hide in the den and sneak upstairs to my room to console me a little. He could have stopped her! He could have been the man in the family and stood up to her! But he didn't. He's a wimp . . . a real wimp. He—just as much as Mother—robbed me of a happy childhood. Mother inflicted the wounds, and he just stood by and watched."

Repressed hatred—hatred she had no idea even existed—surfaced, and Alicia continued the painful process of grieving, forgiving, and taking responsibility for her healing process.

RAGE

Some people keep the clamps on their anger and hatred because they are only too aware of the monster of furious rage that boils within them. When that monster breaks its bonds and explodes—which seldom occurs if they have strong control or often occurs if their control is weakened by added stresses—these people change from Jekyll to Hyde, from numb to passionate, from passive to violent.

> "*Most of the time I'm a good wife and a good mother. I really love my children, but sometimes . . . something snaps. . . .*

"I don't know what happens to me," related Dorothy, confused and depressed. "Most of the time I'm a good wife and a good mother. I really love my children, but sometimes . . . something snaps. . . . Maybe the two year old has spilled something again—usually that's OK, but sometimes . . . my stepson didn't come home last Thursday night and Jim [Dorothy's husband] didn't even care. I woke him up several times in the night to tell him. I didn't sleep a wink—*but he didn't care!* I sat in the bed looking at him. I wanted to hit him so bad! Finally, I . . . I started screaming at him. I wouldn't stop for a long time, and every time he tried to calm me down, I just got madder."

Some people may feel intense hatred toward someone for hurting them (although they may only admit to being "a little bothered" or "frustrated"), but if the threat of expressing their rage toward that person is too great, they displace their anger. One man from a verbally abusive family played sports to "let out some tension," but the competition only reminded him that he couldn't measure up in the eyes of his parents. When he won, he felt superior and arrogant, but when he lost, he violently bashed lockers and trash cans, then wildly speeded off in his car. His case demonstrates that attempts to control rage may be successful in the short-run, but tighter clamps ultimately cause more repression, shame, and denial. This repression leads to a greater reservoir of hatred that will eventually explode in rage.

Many people turn to "pain killers" such as alcohol, drugs, work, food, power, or anything else that promises to cover up the pain of repressed anger. Like other attempts to control anger, these choices also tighten the clamps, creating more pressure, and ironically, assuring more or bigger explosions of uncontrolled rage.

HATING GOD

For many people, the ultimate threat is admitting that they hate God for letting them suffer abuse, humiliation, and emptiness. Their attitude toward Him may be very similar to their attitude toward a parent who failed to protect them. They may not be aware of their anger at God until they are well into the healing process; then their disappointment may be similar to Asaph's as described in Psalm 77. He turned to the Lord for help, but was not comforted.

> In the day of my trouble I sought the Lord;
> In the night my hand was stretched out without weariness;
> My soul refused to be comforted.
> When I remember God, then I am disturbed;
> When I sigh, then my spirit grows faint.
> Thou hast held my eyelids open;
> I am so troubled that I cannot speak (Psalms 77:2–4).

Later, the psalmist reflected on the seeming hopelessness of trusting in God, questioning God's goodness and purposes in his life:

> Will the Lord reject forever?
> And will He never be favorable again?
> Has His lovingkindness ceased forever?
> Has His promise come to an end forever?
> Has God forgotten to be gracious?
> Or has He in anger withdrawn His compassion?
> (Psalms 77:7–9)

Many people feel that God can't be trusted, that He has let them down. They are disappointed in God, and that disappointment is only a short step from blaming Him for their hurt or for not protecting them from being wounded. And that disappointment and blame are only another short step from hate.

"It scares me to even say it," Joseph said cautiously, "but if I'm really honest, I have to admit that I hate God. If He is so powerful and loving, why did He let my parents divorce? Why did He let my dad have a heart attack? Why didn't God cause my folks to love each other . . . and love me? I'm afraid to feel all the rage that I have kept bottled up inside. I'm afraid a bolt of lightning will strike me."

In his book, *Disappointment with God* (Zondervan, 1988), Philip Yancey describes the necessity of being honest *about* God, as well as *with* God. Grieving one's losses includes not only those losses created and allowed by people, but those allowed by God, too. Fear of God's authority may complicate this process, but a patient and wise group leader, friend, or counselor can help sort out the complexities so *all* hurts can be grieved.

THE POWER OF BITTERNESS

Love transforms. So does bitterness. Love stimulates creativity and freshness of thought; it energizes people to care for others and brings affirmation and freedom. Love builds.

. . . Bitterness destroys. It sucks the freshness out of life and focuses attention and efforts on "getting even" and hurting others.

In contrast, bitterness destroys. It sucks the freshness out of life and focuses attention and efforts on "getting even" and hurting others.

Anger's initial motive may be justice. But rather than seeking a just solution that is ultimately constructive, hatred seeks to wound, hurt, humiliate, and destroy. And it is very successful when expressed through verbal and nonverbal condemnation, sarcasm and outright ridicule, attacks and abandonment, and aggressive, passive, and passive-aggressive means.

Jealousy of others' successes is only a half-step away from

hatred. When people compare themselves to others and thus perceive themselves as deficient, the resulting anger can easily turn into hatred—and a desire to hurt the one who has "shown them up."

But in their passion to hurt others, those who lash out in bitterness hurt themselves, too. At the least, they waste precious time on negative, harmful exercises. Usually, though, the tragedy of hatred is much more costly. It consumes people with a passion for revenge that may eventually cause depression or various psychosomatic illnesses.

Frederick Buechner writes:

> Of the Seven Deadly Sins, anger is possibly the most fun. To lick your wounds, to smack your lips over grievances long past, to roll over your tongue the prospect of bitter confrontations still to come, to savor to the last toothsome morsel both the pain you are given and the pain you are giving back—in many ways it is a feast fit for a king. The chief drawback is that what you are wolfing down is yourself. The skeleton at the feast is you.[1]

Admitting hatred is a big step, but it is only one step toward genuine, emotional health. Though they need to keep growing, some people get stuck after this admission.

Blaming others—wanting revenge, holding onto bitterness—gives us a sense of power. We feel in control; we feel "one-up" on those we are blaming. Dealing with our bitterness means much more, then, than admitting we are angry. We need to come to grips with the months or years of nurturing the desire for paying others back. Our wrong—our sin—is not the fact that we are initially angry about what they did to us. When others hurt us, we are genuinely violated. An injustice has occurred. As people made in the image of God, we rightly feel wronged and angry, but when we choose to hold onto our anger with the hope of revenge, we shake our fist at God's sovereignty and goodness. Life, indeed, isn't fair. Recognizing that fact brings health. But *demanding* that the unfairness of life be made right leads us to try to make it right ourselves by punishing the offender. Victims become judges, jurors—and executioners.

When we determine that bitterness and the desire for revenge have been wrong and destructive, we can choose to forgive. (Forgiveness will be covered more fully in a later chapter.) Giving up on revenge, however, takes away our sense of power, our perceived position of being one-up on the other person. We then feel weak, vulnerable, and sad. We grieve instead of resent. We feel a profound sense of loss, but our new vulnerability also leads us to the fertile soil of comfort, love, and hope.

The power of hatred may be broken in an instant, or it may ebb away slowly. Many of us have been taught that we will experience instant joy at our repentance, but joy may come later. First, we must face the very sense of injustice and loss that gave rise to our bitterness. But now, we grieve. The reality of those injustices and losses are staggering for some of us. The immensity of the pain is the very reason for all of our denial and defenses. The healing process takes us to those deep wells again. Most of us hesitate at that point and many of us refuse to drink. We get stuck again. But others have the courage to drink the gall of injustices and wounds, and sooner or later we find the sweetness of peace and true joy.

REFLECTION/DISCUSSION

1. What have you been taught (by parents, teachers, ministers, etc.) about anger, rage, hatred, and bitterness? What aspects of these teachings are true? Which aspects are false, misleading, or incomplete?

2. How does bitterness relate to craving, fear, and shame? For instance, how does fearing someone's disapproval set us up to be hurt by that person and then to hate him?

3. Most Christians have difficulty admitting their intense anger

and hatred. Reflect on sections of this chapter and describe your own feelings and behaviors of:

• Hating yourself

• Hating others

• Rage

• Hating God

4. How has the power of bitterness influenced your life?

5. When is anger justified?

6. Compare and contrast Ephesians 4:26–27 and James 1:20.

7. How does anger become bitterness?

8. Read Ephesians 4:29–32. How can we "put aside" our anger?

9. The psalmists and prophets openly expressed their disappoint-

ment with God. Read Lamentations 3:18. Have you felt this way about God? If so, why?

10. In what ways have hatred and blaming others given you a sense of power?

11. Why is grief an integral part of giving up our bitterness?

[1] Frederich Buechner, *Wishful Thinking: A Theological ABC* (San Francisco: Harper and Row Publishers, 1973), p. 2.

8

---◆---

Ways We Cope

—Robert S. McGee

Even as small children, we build coping systems designed to get the attention we want and block the pain we dread. These systems work to some degree, but ultimately they prevent the very things we need and perpetuate the hurt we fear. Coping mechanisms seem "good enough" until they are overloaded by the excessive weight of desire, fear, shame, and hatred, or until some trauma shocks us into the reality that these mechanisms aren't working for us.

These systems work to some degree, but ultimately they prevent the very things we need and perpetuate the hurt we fear.

We long for our thirst to be quenched, but we are unaware of the "living water" that truly quenches (Isaiah 55:1–3; John 7:37–39). Our expectation that success, pleasure, and approval will meet our deepest needs is an empty hope. Many centuries ago, the Lord spoke of a similar problem among His people: "My people have committed two evils: They have forsaken Me, the fountain of living waters, to hewn for themselves cisterns, broken cisterns, that can hold no water" (Jeremiah 2:13).

Many of us have not been aware that the cisterns we've constructed won't hold water. The influences of our parental models, our siblings and peers, and media have told us that these cisterns are necessary to quench our emotional thirst. Even people who have been Christians for years may have been blinded due to conditioning by their families.

As the healing process begins, we usually recognize our most obvious coping mechanisms. But as the layers of denial are slowly replaced by objectivity, we see more subtle and complex ways we have "gotten by." At each point, we are tempted to believe, *That's it! Now we've finished the process!* Instead we are often shocked, confused, and discouraged to find more layers of denial underneath, along with more hard choices.

The healing process will expose many deeply rooted coping mechanisms. We need to identify these mechanisms over and over again at various levels so we can to develop new patterns. Each observation presents another opportunity to get stuck . . . or to grow.

PATTERNS

The combination of our unmet needs for love, acceptance, and security, our sinful natures and the continued pressures of hurt and anger experienced in dysfunctional families, leads us to all manners of coping. Some of us have develop extreme behavioral and personality disorders, such as psychopathy, sociopathy, and narcissism. But most of our coping behaviors are not so extreme. Rather, our patterns of behavior reflect issues in our lives relating to objectivity, trust, control, responsibility, and facades.

Objectivity—In dysfunctional families, people are not allowed or encouraged to talk about family problems, so objectivity is stunted. We don't have a clear perception of reality. One of the most common maladies of perception is "black and white thinking."

We see people and situations as *all bad* or *all good* instead of observing both strength and weaknesses. We either become totally absorbed in a relationship, or totally reject the person when he falls from the pedestal on which we have placed him. Similarly, we see people as "for us" or "against us." We expect blind loyalty (because that's what *we* give) and we unmercifully condemn those who may slightly disagree with us.

One way to identify a "black-or-white" perception is to consider the pattern of our relationships and our statements about people. Do we typically get very close to others, only to be disappointed in them or rejected by them, and then find others to be close to? Do we tend to describe people as *gray,* or do our descriptions portray people as either *wonderful* or *awful*?

Trust—Some of us have difficulty trusting anyone. Some trust everyone. Our lack of objectivity causes us to blindly trust some people and totally distrust others.

Perhaps we were neglected or abused by our families. We had wanted to trust somebody, but the object of our trust proved unworthy. Yet the threat of being unattached was too threatening, so we learned to blindly trust whoever was available. We clung to that person, even though his attitudes, words, and behavior loudly proclaimed his untrustworthiness.

On the other hand, we may have concluded that no one could be trusted. Even when trustworthy people came into our lives, we were still unable to take the risk of trusting them.

Often, we flip-flop from white to black as our blind faith in someone turns to complete lack of trust. Similarly, on a spiritual level we may also blindly trust God until He disappoints us, then we reject Him as untrustworthy.

To get the others to act in desired ways, controllers have a wide array of techniques, including sarcasm, ridicule, threats, cursing, door slamming, walking away, yelling, silence, withdrawal, and a host of other highly motivating, shame-based, guilt-inducing verbal and nonverbal methods.

Control—People in dysfunctional families use control rather than love and respect as they relate to each other. To get the others to act in desired ways, controllers have a wide array of techniques, including sarcasm, ridicule, threats, cursing, door slamming, walking away, yelling, silence, withdrawal, and a host of other highly motivating, shame-based, guilt-inducing verbal and non-verbal methods. They may use praise and rewards—not to value the other person, but to manipulate and reinforce behavior they want that person to display.

In such an environment, many of us lose our sense of identity. We become puppets, dancing to another's desires as our strings are pulled. We want to avoid rejection and gain approval so badly that we learn to read others' minds, interpret their gestures, and do what they want even if they don't say a word. In fact, if they have to ask, we've failed them. The notion of saying no becomes a completely foreign idea.

A controlling person takes satisfaction in the acquiescence of some people, and surprisingly in the rebellion of others. When a person says, "I'm not going to do what Dad wants, no matter what!" his attitude and actions are still being controlled by his father. He isn't making his own choice; he is reacting.

Yet giving in and giving up are also ways of controlling others, too. When we give in to make others happy with us, we are trying to control their behavior. Acquiescence may not appear to be controlling, but its goal is to get a person to love and care and approve. Similarly, rebellion is an attempt to control others, by punishing them and making them unhappy and worried.

Responsibility—When we try to control others instead of letting them "own" their individual feelings and behavior, we are being overly responsible. And when we let their behavior and attitudes control our happiness and actions, we are avoiding responsibility for our feelings and behaviors. We are then irresponsible.

One of the great, continual tasks in life is to determine what we are responsible for. Those of us from dysfunctional families have an inherent disadvantage: we have a warped view of responsibility. In some relationships, we occasionally feel like an indispensable "savior." It is up to us, we believe, to make people happy, successful, and good. If irresponsible people let us act in that role, then we feel great and keep coming to the rescue. If we fail or if we don't try, we feel like a "Judas" who has betrayed those who trusted and needed us.

The issue of responsibility, like control, is an area where many people lose their identity. We learn to feel what others want us to feel, say what they want us to say, and do what they want us to do. We feel so responsible to measure up and to please them that we lose the capacity to be ourselves.

Facades—With unmet needs for love and security, inability to know who to trust, and fuzzy boundaries of responsibility, we play games. We develop a facade, projecting to others (and ourselves) the image of the person we want to be. We may or may not be successful.

We may try to project confidence, but our behavior may actually be boorish and obnoxious. Or our attempts to be warm may seem insincere to others. Some of us, however, are so good at playing this game, that we fool ourselves into believing we are really as confident, secure, and gifted as we appear. Some of the most proficient "actors" have the hardest time recognizing their phoniness. They've gotten too many strokes and been reinforced too frequently to doubt themselves.

As a person progresses in the healing process, he begins to recognize the facade on which he has built his relationships . . . and the emptiness and loneliness underneath. Recently in a support group, a woman told us, "I used to know exactly what I wanted and where I was going with my life, but it was all a cover . . . a lie. I was using my drives and abilities and relationships to hide from the hurt. Now I'm confused. I see that all of that is superficial, but I feel empty. If I'm not the person I used to be, who am I?"

To help keep up the facade, we use various defense mechanisms and drives. The defense mechanisms are designed primarily to protect us from hurt. The drives are attempts to gain respect and approval. These overlap and interrelate, but we will differentiate them here for the sake of clarity. Most of us find that several of these seem to work best for us.

DEFENSE MECHANISMS

Several techniques we use to keep from experiencing pain in our relationships are shown on the following pages.

Suppression—One of the most common defenses used to block hurt involves "stuffing" the emotions to prevent feeling them. Even if we recall an experience of being abused, we learn to relate it without any emotion at all, numb to the hurt and anger.

Repression—We can stuff the emotions to the point of forgetting the event which caused them. This is repression. "I don't know what happened after Mom and Dad divorced," someone might say. "I don't remember much for several years after that."

Denial is redefining reality to make another person's neglect and abuse appear to be love and respect.

Denial—"I'm sure my brother cares about me. It wasn't really stealing. He needed the money. That's why he took it from me." Denial is redefining reality to make another person's neglect and abuse appear to be love and respect.

Rationalization—Rationalization is the explaining away of our own sins and mistakes. We then avoid responsibility for our behaviors. "There are lots of good reasons why I got an abortion," a young woman told me. "And I don't feel guilty at all."

Projection—Since our own motives are not healthy, we assume others' aren't either. We project our own feelings to the other person. "I hate him because he's so selfish," a woman retorted about her husband, though the man had spent his life trying to please this demanding woman and only rarely did anything for himself.

Transference—Similarly, when we have suffered at the hands of one person, we may transfer our feelings about that person to others we know. One man was bitter toward his father, and he automatically assumed that every authority figure (pastor, employer, God, etc.) was just like his abusive dad. Without analyzing the trustworthiness of each individual, he treated them all with disdain and contempt.

Displaced Anger—John got angry at the machinery he worked on. Did the lawn mower call him a dirty name? No, the source of his anger was his mother, but he was too threatened to be angry with her. Instead, he got angry at something that was less intimidating.

Substitutionary Anger—Many of us allow ourselves to feel anger to cover for the hurt we really feel. We intrinsically believe that rage, outbursts, and rebellious behavior are more palatable and less threatening to us than hurt. We may feel shame, depression, and self-hatred because of these explosions of anger, but those things still seem better than facing the ugly reality of deep wounds caused by others.

Addictions—Physiological addictions to alcohol, drugs, and TV are primarily ways to escape reality and to numb pain. Psychological addictions to food, sex, gambling, and any other "good thing turned bad" combine both the escape from reality and the drive for fulfillment.

Depression/Passivity—Sometimes depression is physiological, caused by a brain tumor or some other physical problem. But more frequently the source is repressed anger or a deep sense of loss. Depression is an involuntary defense mechanism to prevent more feelings of hurt and anger. Passivity, which may accompany depression, is also a means to control risks and minimize hurt in tasks and relationships.

DRIVES

Most of us combine various defense mechanisms with the compulsion to do whatever it takes to win the love, security, and respect we desperately want.

Success—"All my life I've climbed the ladder of success, only to find it leaning against the wrong wall," stated a very successful Dallas businessman. We believe that wealth, beauty, prestige, positions, titles, and possessions will fulfill our deepest needs and fill the void in our lives—and for a short time they do. We compare ourselves with peers, hoping to "measure up" and "come out on top" or at least at a respectable level. We set high standards and rigorously try to meet them, but live in fear of failure.

Pleasure—"If only I could go on a cruise, I'd be happy! If only I could have that house (or car, or wardrobe, or whatever), I'd be satisfied. If only I could go to bed with him, I would feel wanted and loved." Pleasure for some means excitement. For others, it signifies a quiet, restful place or being around people who make us feel good. They do make us feel good—for a while. But the end result is emptiness.

> *Virtually every TV commercial and magazine ad is designed to convince us that the product or service offered will enable us to get the respect, admiration, and affection we crave.*

Approval—Above all, we want to be loved. If we can't have love, we will settle for respect. Virtually every TV commercial and magazine ad is designed to convince us that the product or service offered will enable us to get the respect, admiration, and affection we crave. We want approval so much that we sacrifice ourselves— our desires, goals, feelings, integrity, and honesty—in the attempt to win it.

The patterns we develop, the defense mechanisms, and the desires to gain success, pleasure, and approval are deeply ingrained in us. They are modeled by our families, the media, schools, and too often, even our churches. The "system" rewards those who play the game best: those who block their pain and earn enough approval to keep going, those who control others even as they are being controlled in a pathological family ballet, and those who are "clever" enough to avoid being honest about their hurt so they can continue living with the facade securely in place.

Emotional healing requires that we identify our defenses and drives. If we are blindsided by them, we will probably be confused, hurt, angry, and stuck.

REFLECTION/DISCUSSION
Patterns:
1. Describe your life's pattern in each of these areas:

   • Trust

   • Control

   • Responsibility

   • Facades

2. Describe how you have used each of these defense mechanisms to block pain. (Note: You probably use some more than others.)

   • Suppression

   • Repression

   • Denial

   • Rationalization

   • Projection

   • Transference

   • Displaced Anger

   • Substitutionary Anger

   • Addictions

   • Depression/Passivity

3. Describe how you have used drives to gain respect and approval.

   • Success

   • Pleasure

• Approval

4. Success, pleasure, and approval seem to promise us fulfillment, but they ultimately fail. Reflect on these passages and
   questions:

SUCCESS

   Read Luke 22:24–27. How does Jesus define greatness?
How does the world define greatness?

PLEASURE

   Read Luke 12:15–21. What did the rich man seek? Why was
he foolish?

APPROVAL

   Read Luke 14:7–11. What are some ways we "take the place
of honor"? Why do we seek honor?

9

◆

A Penchant for Justice

—Pat Springle

Vɪᴄᴛɪᴍꜱ ᴏꜰ ᴀʙᴜꜱᴇ, whether physical or emotional, begin to develop a different perspective of the world. After being deeply wounded often enough, they give up on expecting to receive love or goodness. They cling instead to an insistence on justice being served.

After being deeply wounded often enough, victims give up on expecting to receive love or goodness. They cling instead to an insistence on justice being served.

They intuitively develop a scale in their lives by which they weigh events. They hope to discover a balance of enough good things happening to them and enough punishment inflicted on the ones who have made them victims. But their long past of being victimized usually makes the thirst for justice unquenchable. No matter how many good things happen to them, they never seem to be satisfied. No matter how much punishment is inflicted on the ones who have harmed them, it's not enough.

And of course, life doesn't dole out unending streams of good for victims or condemnation for selfish and manipulative people. Every heartache or failure for the victim is a new wound. Every time the perpetrator prospers, the scale screams of more injustice. The bitterness inherent in this demand for justice then continues to be nourished. The victim becomes more demanding, more angry, and more bitter.

"What did I do to deserve this?" a lady almost yelled as she told me her story of continuous verbal abuse from her father. "I was just a little girl! Why did he keep saying those terrible, condemning things to me? Couldn't he see he was killing me?" As we talked during the next several weeks, she told me she often fantasized about her father being killed, dying some slow painful death.

"I know I shouldn't feel this way. . . . I'm a Christian and I know I should love him, but I hate him for all he did to me." She then described all the problems of her life: her fear of authority, constant tension in her marriage, bouts of depression, struggles with her daughter, and on and on. "If it weren't for him, I wouldn't have all these problems," she said bitterly.

Her bitterness and constant blaming was not limited to her father. She blamed somebody for everything that was wrong with her life. Her hair-trigger response of blame was set off by the least offense, whether real or perceived. Her family was most often under attack, but she also internalized blame and felt severe self-hatred.

Her thirst for justice caused her to see people and circumstances as "all good" or "all bad." People generally started on the plus side of her ledger, and were considered wonderful people, "the best friends in the world," or "somebody I can really count on." But then they would hurt her or let her down and plunge to the negative side. She would then look for a new person to fill the gap in the "all good" category, and the cycle would continue. Those who see themselves as victims are hard people to live with, and they very likely find it difficult to live with themselves.

THE "VICTIM MENTALITY"

A victim's insistence on justice grows out of a mixture of perceptions—many of which are based on past truth and half-truth. Yet the person is full of assumptions about future relationships. The "victim mentality" is characterized by a combination of the following assumptions.

"They're out to get me."—The pain in the person's past is very real, and those wounds often lead to a subtle paranoia for the future. Victims feel that people—especially those who have inflicted pain in the past—desire to hurt them again.

"Nobody understands me."—Victims feel lonely and abandoned. They believe that no one understands their pain. (However, this sense of isolation can lead to absorbing relationships if the victim finds someone who can understand and identify with the victimization.)

"My problems are your fault."—Though others may indeed be responsible for much pain, victims typically blame virtually *all* their problems on others. This shifting of responsibility makes them vulnerable to additional pain when people "don't come through" as they anticipate.

The "Victim Mentality"
"They're out to get me."
"Nobody understands me."
"My problems are your fault."
"It'll never change."
"I have to be right."
"I have to punish him."
"I deserve for things to go well."

"It'll never change."—Victims may loudly express a desire for change in their situations, but many have reached a state of hopelessness. They have ceased to believe that life will ever be different. This hopelessness may be true depression, or it may be a way to exert power over others, manipulating them through self-pity.

"I have to be right."—The penchant for justice leaves little room to admit wrongs and errors. Most victims are terribly threatened to even consider that they might be wrong. They are quite insecure and feel that being wrong will transfer much-needed points from the plus side of their scale to the negative side.

"I have to punish him."—Deeply wounded people often experience a double whammy of feelings: the compulsion to punish offenders, and guilt for thinking such things. They believe that no one else will serve justice, so they have to punish by either aggressive or passive-aggressive behavior. But if they do anything which genuinely hurts the offending person, they may feel guilt, shame, and self-condemnation. (Sometimes they feel these things even when they only *think* of hurting someone.)

"I deserve for things to go well."—The expectation for the scales to be balanced is reflected in the attitude that we have somehow earned the right for people to treat us nicely. This way of thinking leads to cycles of feeling "up" or "down" depending on the perceived fairness of circumstances and people.

A Two-Edged Sword

"I lived with a constant fear that I wouldn't get what I deserved."

One woman told me, "All my life, I've felt that somebody— God, my family, or someone—owes me something to make up for all the hurt I've experienced. Whenever things went well, I felt vindicated. Not happy, really, but vindicated. Happiness and vindication are different: one is relaxed and content; the other is proud and defiant. I lived with a constant fear that I wouldn't get what I deserved. I tested people to see if they were 'for me or against me.' When something didn't go well, or when people didn't give me the attention I 'deserved' (or demanded!), I felt like the old wound was torn open again. So many situations and people seemed unfair because I demanded so much from them. I expected them to balance the scales of justice and to give me the love and contentment I really wanted. Demanding what I 'deserved' seemed right and fair, but it was unrealistic. It led to more bitterness and resentment if my needs weren't met, and pride and greater demands if they were."

Of course, most people with a victim mentality are unaware that these perceptions are full of half-truths and presuppositions. Their perceived observations *feel* like reality. They *seem* like the gospel truth. And formed after years of developing a mental and emotional framework, they are not easily recognized or changed.

Victims can't stand injustice, but neither can they enjoy the good things in life. Their bitterness toward others and intense, internalized blame prevent them from feeling good. They crave satisfaction, but it escapes them.

One young man told me that he desperately wants to be loved and to "make up for all the bad things" that have happened to him. "But when good things happen to me, I don't have emotional shelves to put them on. They fall on the floor and shatter. I want them so much, but I can't have them."

The penchant for justice is a two-edged sword. Though we demand it for those who have hurt us, we won't admit that if *we* received justice, we would be in trouble! Our focus is generally on those who have wronged us instead of our sins toward others. If we are truly objective, however, we must realize that we are not only victims, but victimizers as well.

If we insist on justice and punishment for others, we should also take a look at our own sinfulness and the justice that is demanded for our sins. If, however, we believe that all our problems (and sins) are someone else's fault, we will continue to demand justice and condemn others instead of taking responsibility for ourselves and becoming more merciful.

OUR VIEW OF GOD

Victims almost universally transfer their problems with earthly authorities (particularly parents) to their relationships with God. If parents have been harsh and abusive, they conclude that God is also demanding. If parents have been aloof and neglectful, they assume God is uncaring and untrustworthy. These people may be able to clearly articulate the theology of the unconditional love and acceptance of God based on biblical doctrines such as justification and reconciliation, but their most deeply held convictions are just the opposite. The mental and emotional grid they have established consists of beliefs such as:

- *God isn't fair.*

- *If God is all-powerful, He could have stopped the abuse I've experienced. Since He didn't, He either must not care or must not be strong enough to help.*

- *He won't/can't come through for me when I need Him.*

- *I have to do everything just right for Him to help me.*

- *He's using the abuse to punish me for something I did.*

- *I know what I need, and if He doesn't provide what I need, He isn't trustworthy.*

The psalmist, Asaph, felt that he was a victim of God's untrustworthiness. In Psalm 73, Asaph recounts his perspective of wicked people prospering while good people (like himself) suffered. He was confused and angry. He concluded:

> They are not in trouble as other men;
> Nor are they plagued like mankind.
> Therefore pride is their necklace;
> The garment of violence covers them.
> Their eye bulges from fatness;
> The imaginations of their heart run riot. . . .
> Surely in vain I have kept my heart pure,
> And washed my hands in innocence (Psalms 73:5–7, 13).

Later, Asaph understood that God would ultimately balance the scales in His way and in His timing. He recalled his intense anger and God's patience with him during his anger:

> When my heart was embittered,
> And I was pierced within,
> Then I was senseless and ignorant;

I was like a beast before Thee.
Nevertheless I am continually with Thee;
Thou hast taken hold of my right hand.
With Thy counsel Thou wilt guide me,
And afterward receive me to glory (Psalms 73:21–24).

In another passage of Scripture, the prophet Isaiah observes the complaining and blaming attitudes of God's people. When they felt they were victims of God's unfairness toward them, Isaiah asked a penetrating question: "Why do you say, O Jacob, and assert, O Israel, 'My way is hidden from the Lord, and the justice due me escapes the notice of my God?'" (Isaiah 40:27)

The prophet responded to his own question:

Do you not know? Have you not heard? The Everlasting God, the Lord, the Creator of the ends of the earth does not become weary or tired. His understanding is inscrutable. He gives strength to the weary, and to him who lacks might He increases power (Isaiah 40:28–29).

Isaiah's questions, "Do you not know? Have you not heard?" are a stinging rebuke to the people. They had seen God rescue them from slavery in Egypt, provide food for them for 40 years in the wilderness after they had refused to trust Him, lead them to the Promised Land, provide leaders and land for them to enjoy, rescue them from self-induced calamity time after time, and provide them with sacred Scriptures and traditions to remind them of His kindness and strength. So the implication in Isaiah's questions is, *You have experienced so much of God's grace, you certainly* should *know, and you certainly* have *heard.*

A THREE-LEGGED STOOL

God knows, He cares, and He is strong enough to accomplish His purposes.

All of God's actions had shown the people of Israel that He is good, powerful, and sovereign. God knows, He cares, and He is strong enough to accomplish His purposes.

Victims need to grasp all three of these truths about God's character. Like the legs of a three-legged stool, all are required for stability. Some people don't believe any of these! Others believe that God is good, but that He can't accomplish His purposes because He isn't strong enough or doesn't know what to do. Others may believe that He is powerful, but whimsical, and plays games with our lives.

The Bible is full of passages which describe the attributes of God, but that doesn't mean that it is a simple matter to understand how God works in every specific situation. Perhaps the sovereignty of God is the most difficult for victims to grasp. "Does He really know what He's doing?" they ask, and, "If He does, why in the world does He let me hurt like this?"

These questions have no easy answers. We cannot presume to comprehend the depths of the mind of God. He allows events and relationships which seem horribly unfair and un-God-like to us. Perhaps our comfort lies not in understanding His particular purposes, but in trusting His basic character.

A friend once said, "I'm realizing that I will never understand all the 'whys' of life. I'm coming to grips with the fact that life is unfair. I don't like it that way; I wish I could count on all the books being balanced every day (or week or year or lifetime)! But I can rely on the fact that God knows what He's doing. Even when things look way out of line and unfair, I can trust that He knows, He cares, and that He is powerful enough to accomplish His purposes."

Sooner or later, we must come to grips with the unfairness of life. We need to throw away our scales and seek instead a deeper and richer knowledge of the One who is both loving and wise. Then we can grieve our losses instead of demanding that they be made good.

The sense of loss is real. It hurts. But demanding that these losses be righted will only lead to more bitterness and pain. Deep wounds such as not feeling loved as a child, not feeling valued, not being comforted, being betrayed by a spouse or a child, or any of a myriad of others are not easy to face and grieve. We need the comforting and healing environment of loving people communicating the grace of a loving God. As we grieve the losses of the past, we will also learn to grieve the losses of each day. The pattern of our lives will change from holding out for unrealistic demands to accepting, grieving, and enjoying what is real.

STEPS OF PROGRESS

1. RECOGNIZE YOUR "VICTIM MENTALITY."
2. LEAVE VENGEANCE TO GOD.
3. REFLECT ON GOD'S GOODNESS, POWER, AND SOVEREIGNTY.
4. FORGIVE THOSE WHO HAVE HURT YOU.
5. CLARIFY YOUR RESPONSIBILITIES.
6. CONTINUE TO FOCUS ON GOD'S CHARACTER.

Developing trust in the hard-to-understand character of God is a big step for victims, but this trust is essential if we are to avoid getting stuck in the healing process. Here are several steps to help move from demanding justice to enjoying mercy.

Recognize your "victim mentality"—Learn to identify particular thoughts and feelings which reflect a victim mentality. As you identify these thoughts, you will then be able to understand why you think, feel, and act the way you do.

Leave vengeance to God—The Lord has not assigned us the responsibility (or given us the right) of taking revenge on others. We can and should develop a biblical identity with corresponding healthy boundaries and choices, but taking revenge is sin. Paul wrote the believers in Rome: "Never take your own revenge, beloved, but leave room for the wrath of God, for it is written, 'Vengeance is Mine, I will repay,' says the Lord" (Romans 12:19). God will make things right in His way and in His time. We need to avoid complicating the issue by getting in the way.

Reflect on God's goodness, power, and sovereignty—Victims struggle with at least one of these aspects of God's character. As we reflect on His true character and talk to others about it, we may realize that we believe even less than we thought we did! That realization may be quite confusing and disconcerting at first, but it provides an opportunity for real growth.

Forgive those who have hurt you—As you reflect on God's love and His forgiveness of your sins, you will be more motivated to forgive others who have sinned against you. Paul wrote the Colossians: ". . . bearing with one another, and forgiving each other, whoever has a complaint against anyone; just as the Lord forgave you, so also should you" (Colossians 3:13).

Clarify your responsibilities—Victims often expect others to be responsible for making them happy. In fact, victims demand that others do good things for them as a means of balancing the scales. We must realize that God is inscrutable, that He will ultimately balance the scales Himself, and that we can stop demanding that others take care of us emotionally. Then we can begin to be responsible for our own feelings, behaviors, and desires.

Continue to focus on God's character—As the healing process continues, the Lord carries us through many cycles of understanding, grieving, forgiving, and taking responsibility for ourselves. We may feel stuck when we uncover wounds which have been hidden for years. We may even feel that our healing is going backward, but these are new opportunities to apply the truths and principles we have already learned: God is good; God is powerful; God is sovereign.

Another place victims often get stuck is between feeling the intense hurt and anger they have repressed and making good choices in their lives and relationships. Grieving and taking responsibility are major issues in the healing process. In the next chapter, we will examine the interplay of these issues.

REFLECTION/DISCUSSION
Review the six steps and answer the following questions.

1.   In what ways do you feel, think, and act like a victim? In what ways are you *actually* a victim?

2. List ways that people take revenge on others (including gossip!) or try to punish people, either aggressively or passive-aggressively. Which of these do you use?

3. Which passages of Scripture (in this chapter) are most helpful to you? Why?

4. How does reflecting on God's forgiveness of your sins help you forgive those who have wounded you?

5. In what areas of your life (time, finances, feelings, choices, etc.) have you expected others to take care of you?

What is your responsibility in each of these areas?

How will you make the proper choices from now on?

6. What environment do you need (an encouraging relationship, time, reflection, etc.) to help you continue to grow in God's love and strength?

Section Two

10

$\blacklozenge$

Grief
and
Responsibility

—Pat Springle

THE ROAD TO EMOTIONAL HEALING involves grief and responsibility. Both. Not either/or. Genuine emotional, spiritual, and relational healing involves grieving past wounds *and* taking responsibility for our own behavior. Many people overemphasize one or the other. Or worse, they condemn people who are trying to find that balance. Serious difficulties remain, however, for those who fail to embrace both grief and responsibility.

RESPONSIBILITY WITHOUT GRIEF

"Forget the past."

"Move on."

"Forgive and forget."

These are some of the many admonitions from those who stress personal responsibility without understanding the need to grieve losses. Some people don't understand the level of pain within abusive families and the need to deal with wounds that have been inflicted. Others hide behind simplistic platitudes because they are afraid of dealing with their own pain.

In a Sunday School class, someone who had been reading books on emotional healing asked how a passage in Ephesians related to emotional development. The teacher pounced like he had been waiting for someone to ask that question. He retorted, "I've heard a lot on the radio about 'emotional healing,' but the Bible never even mentions it. All this stuff about dealing with the past is hogwash. In fact, Paul wrote in Philippians 3:13: 'Forgetting what lies behind and pressing forward to what lies ahead. . . .' So we need to just forget the past like Paul says."

The person in the class was offended by the teacher's dogmatic reaction, but she calmly asked, "Why is there so much in the Bible about comfort if pain isn't a reality? It seems that a person probably can't forget the past if its wounds still haunt him."

The teacher was unimpressed by her reasoning. "All I know is what the Bible says, and Paul says to forget the past. I, for one, intend to be obedient to that."

Many of us are quite susceptible to control and manipulation because of the wounds of the past. Some leaders skillfully use guilt to prod us to "be responsible" to do what they want us to do: giving, serving, fasting, attending services, witnessing, daily devotions, teaching toddlers, cooking for shut-ins, and a host of other good deeds. We live by their imposed "oughts" and "shoulds," trying to do all we can. Then, we think, maybe we will have our deepest needs met. Then, maybe we will be accepted.

The American church today is filled with wounded people who either have given up and become irresponsible or, due to their need for acceptance, have become overly responsible and do whatever others say is necessary.

A person with a broken arm needs to give it special attention for a period of time so the arm can be strengthened and wholeness restored.

Wounded people need to be responsible, but they should first focus their responsibility on finding healing for themselves, not performing for others. Emotional wounds are not unlike physical wounds in one sense. A person with a broken arm needs to give it special attention for a period of time so the arm can be strengthened and wholeness restored. If he neglects the wound and keeps performing all his usual tasks, the arm may become severely impaired. Disease can set in. Any short-term gains of performance are greatly offset by long-term disabilities.

We live in an instant society. We don't like to wait. We want to be comfortable. So we conclude that pain, especially over a long period of time, is bad. We've been trained that we can have what we want quickly and painlessly. It is no wonder that dealing with the pains of the past is considered a nuisance at best, and may even be seen as unbiblical.

GRIEF WITHOUT RESPONSIBILITY

Refusing to grieve as you try to be responsible causes problems, but grieving the past without taking responsibility is just as unbalanced. It is very difficult for abused people to break through their denial and come to grips with their pain, loneliness, hatred, and shame. When they do, it is often overwhelming. They feel victimized. They often indulge in self-pity and blame the offenders.

Feeling self-pity and shock at the reality of being abused is a very common phenomenon in the healing process. It is an important step because many of us are, in fact, victims. But if we do not move through this stage and take responsibility for our own lives, we will be stuck in grief, continuously bogged down in feeling sorry for ourselves and blaming others for the "terrible fix" we are in.

Kim had been sexually abused by her uncle between the ages of 10 and 13. She grew up, got married, and eventually her husband observed some peculiar behaviors which he finally decided to ask her about. His questions were met with a wall of defensiveness. And after several icy months in their relationship, they went to a marriage counselor at their church. The counselor realized something lay hidden in Kim's life, so she suggested that Kim meet with her alone.

During the course of several months of sessions, Kim began to remember what happened. She had a few flashbacks. She felt overwhelmed—devastated by the resurfacing memories. For the next six months, Kim seemed to make very little progress, except for the fact that her shock had turned to hatred toward her uncle and her parents—who probably knew about the abuse but had done nothing to protect her.

From the outset, the counselor realized that overcoming denial would be a major step—actually a long series of steps—and she encouraged Kim to continue her progress. At one point, she told Kim, "Yes, you are a victim—a victim of your uncle, your mother, and your father. They wronged you terribly, but you need not remain a victim. You can take responsibility to go on from here and experience healing and wholeness." At each counseling session, she tried to help Kim understand the steps she still needed to take, but Kim's hatred overshadowed everything. At this writing, Kim is still stuck in her grief, and sees her counselor only irregularly. She feels like a victim because she *is* one. But she has not taken the steps necessary to move beyond victimization, develop a healthy self-esteem, or build healthy relationships—even with a husband who loves her.

BALANCE

Few of us can find the proper balance of grief and responsibility for ourselves. We need others' help and objectivity. I remember plenty of times when I thought I was taking huge steps of personal responsibility to escape manipulation, but a close friend said they weren't big enough.

"You're kidding!" I remember telling him. "I've never been this honest with someone in my life!"

"Yes," he responded calmly, "but think about it. What is reality? How do you really feel?"

"But I can't say all that!"

"Why not?"

"Because she would get really angry at me."

"So . . . listen to what you just said."

"Well, she would . . . but I guess . . . so you think I'm still setting myself up to be manipulated, don't you?"

"What do you think?"

"Okay, but I haven't done this very much. What does it mean to 'be honest' without hurting others?"

"For one thing it doesn't mean that you don't hurt others. It means that you love them enough to be honest with them. Hiding isn't loving them, but attacking isn't either. Genuine love motivates us to be honest, but also how, when, and where to communicate the truth. If we avoid the truth or if we use truth to attack, we are only being manipulative to get what we want. Loving communication has the other person's best interests in mind."

"You mean that if I am honest, I can let people respond however they want to? And changing what I say and do to avoid getting them angry is manipulation?"

At that point a light came on for me and I continued to take steps toward emotional healing. Without friends who encourage us to balance our grief with responsibility, we tend to remain stuck in anger and self-pity, still trying to earn self-respect by performing for others and avoiding pain every way we can.

We need relationships with people who know how to grieve *and* show responsibility for themselves. We need people who are sounding boards for our thoughts, who provide loving and constructive feedback, and who genuinely care. The balance is awkward and difficult for all of us—like learning to ride a bicycle—and we need to find people who will help us.

Some of us have difficulty finding people we trust. Our personal contacts may have broken confidences or betrayed us in some other way. Support groups might make us feel uncomfortable, since we don't know the people there. But sometimes the problem is that we are searching for an individual or a group who will tell us what we *want* to hear—*that we don't really have problems after all*. If so, we aren't seeking honest relationships yet.

Be honest about your fears and take a few risks. You may be disappointed with someone who has promised to help, but doesn't. You may need to look for others. But don't give up until you find somebody!

MODELS OF GRIEF

Several months ago I was leading a small group. As I began to talk about the healing process and the necessity of grieving our losses, a lady asked, "What do you mean, 'grieving our losses'? Did somebody die or something? What losses are you talking about?"

Good questions. Many people equate grief with death, but death is only one of many losses we all experience. Our losses can be mundane (losing a car key, spilling orange juice, being late for an appointment), significant (losing a job, being rejected by peers, a broken arm), or severe (the death of a close friend, parent, sibling, spouse, or child). Emotional abuse and neglect can fall into any of these categories, depending on the severity of the wounds inflicted.

Many abused people compare their sense of loss to a death. "It's like part of me died," one man said. "The little boy in me who wanted to be loved and accepted died. He was killed by the abuse of his alcoholic father and neglectful, aloof mother. I know I'm still alive, but the idea—the dream of growing up in a happy home—is dead."

The Scriptures are full of comfort for those who have experienced (or who fear) loss in their lives. The Bible addresses the full spectrum of human grief experiences.

If you feel empty and lonely, with no comfort, you're in good company:

> I have heard many such things; sorry comforters are you all (Job 16:2).

> Reproach has broken my heart, and I am so sick. And I looked for sympathy, but there was none, and for comforters, but I found none (Psalms 69:20).

> They have heard that I groan; there is no one to comfort me; all my enemies have heard of my calamity; they are glad that Thou hast done it. Oh, that Thou wouldst bring the day which Thou hast proclaimed, that they may become like me (Lamentations 1:21).

Yet Scripture does promise comfort, even during the worst of times. In the Bible's most familiar psalm, David acknowledges the comforting presence and direction of God in the midst of his fears of being hurt:

> Even though I walk through the valley of the shadow of death, I fear no evil; for Thou art with me; Thy rod and Thy staff, they comfort me (Psalms 23:4).

Paul, the great church leader, was certainly no stranger to abuse:

> Are they servants of Christ? (I speak as if insane) I more so; in far more labors, in far more imprisonments, beaten times without number, often in danger of death.
> Five times I received from the Jews thirty-nine lashes. Three times I was beaten with rods, once I was stoned, three times I was shipwrecked, a night and a day I have spent in the deep.
> have been on frequent journeys, in dangers from rivers, dangers from robbers, dangers from my countrymen, dangers from the Gentiles, dangers in the city, dangers in the wilderness, dangers on the sea, dangers among false brethren;
> I have been in labor and hardship, through many sleepless nights, in hunger and thirst, often without food, in cold and exposure.
> Apart from such external things, there is the daily pressure upon me of concern for all the churches (2 Corinthians 11:23-28).

But through all these wounds at the hands of others, Paul experienced God's comfort. He was so convinced of the power of God's comforting hand that he could pray:

> Now may our Lord Jesus Christ Himself and God our Father, who has loved us and given us eternal comfort and good hope by grace,
> Comfort and strengthen your hearts in every good work and word (2 Thessalonians 2:16–17).

Paul also acknowledged that God's people are often the instruments of comfort in our lives. During a particularly trying time in his life, his friend, Titus, came to comfort him. Of this experience, Paul wrote:

> God, who comforts the depressed, comforted us by the coming of Titus;

And not only by his coming, but also by the comfort with which he was comforted in you, as he reported to us your longing, your mourning, your zeal for me; so that I rejoiced even more (2 Corinthians 7:6–7).

Another aspect of grief is the genuine remorse we feel for our sins and the ways we have wounded others.

Another aspect of grief is the genuine remorse we feel for our sins and the ways we have wounded others. Most of us first experience the extremes of either denial or self-hatred in response to our sins. But as perception and stability grow, we should develop more of a "godly sorrow" (2 Corinthians 7:9–10) and healthy remorse for our sins (Psalms 32 and 51). God's forgiveness is vast and deep. His grace makes it possible for us to be honest about our sins. We can then face the consequences of those sins and genuinely grieve over them in a way that minimizes neither our offense nor His grace.

Many authorities have observed stages in the grief process, and they have developed models to help people better understand their progress through these stages. These models vary from simple to complex, and they differ somewhat in regard to the type of loss. For instance, a terminally ill cancer patient's grief over his impending death may be significantly different from the sudden and overwhelming shock of a person whose spouse is killed in a car wreck. Those who have been emotionally abused or neglected usually grieve more like the cancer patient than the spouse of the crash victim.

Perhaps the best known model for grief is found in Elisabeth Kübler-Ross's book, *On Death and Dying*.[1] She noticed that terminally ill cancer patients consistently tend to move through the five stages of denial, anger, bargaining, grief, and acceptance. Many psychologists have also observed these stages in their work with emotionally traumatized people.[2]

John W. James and Frank Cherry, cofounders of The Grief Recovery Institute, take a different approach. They focus on the person's responsibility rather than the emotions of the grieving process, and they describe five distinct stages in their book, *The Grief Recovery Handbook*.[3] These include:

1. Gaining Awareness
2. Accepting Responsibility
3. Identifying Recovery Communication
4. Taking Actions
5. Moving Beyond Loss

This sense of responsibility detailed by James and Cherry enables us to be honest about our confusion, hurt, and anger as we grieve.

In a more expansive list of grief process characteristics, the authors of *The Grief Adjustment Guide* outline two ends of a long continuum: Loss-Hurt, the beginning of the process, and Loss-Adjustment, the conclusion of that process.[4] The characteristics between these ends include:

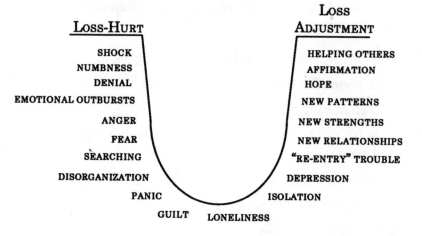

LOSS-HURT

SHOCK
NUMBNESS
DENIAL
EMOTIONAL OUTBURSTS
ANGER
FEAR
SEARCHING
DISORGANIZATION
PANIC
GUILT   LONELINESS

LOSS ADJUSTMENT

HELPING OTHERS
AFFIRMATION
HOPE
NEW PATTERNS
NEW STRENGTHS
NEW RELATIONSHIPS
"RE-ENTRY" TROUBLE
DEPRESSION
ISOLATION

All of those who create models for the grieving process explain that the stages are quite fluid. People go through the process in different ways at different speeds for different reasons. And whatever model you prefer, the conclusion is that grief is, indeed, a process. It involves honesty about the loss, time to experience sadness and renewal, and responsibility to take action. To quote Rusty Berkus from *The Grief Adjustment Guide*, "There is no *right* way to grieve—there is just *your* way."[5]

TAKING RESPONSIBILITY

A woman had been a victim of neglect from one parent and smothering from the other. Her brothers had made fun of her so often that she was scarred from their verbal jabs. Yet she was ready to take responsibility for her life. She affirmed, "I am a victim of others' irresponsibility. I wish I had been treated differently. I wish I had been loved, and I wish I could have felt secure and happy. But now I've got to grow up. I've got to make my own decisions. Nobody can do that for me. It's up to me." There was a blend of anger, confusion, hope, despair, and resolution in her voice at different times. "What do I do now?" she asked.

The actions we need to take in such cases are very likely the opposite of those we have been using to gain approval and cover up pain. The primary decisions we need to make concern relationships.

We should take responsibility to put ourselves in a nurturing environment. We need to receive (and give) honesty, sincerity, and love. And we should realize that while this environment will not be perfect, it should be dynamic. With the encouragement of others in the process, we can take responsibility to:

- Feel our feelings instead of suppressing them

- Talk about the family secret instead of hiding it

- Remember long-buried events

- Stop fixing others by trying to make them happy, successful, and good

- Start taking care of our own needs

- Develop trust instead of fear

- Tell people the truth

- Set boundaries in relationships

- Have fun instead of feeling guilty for relaxing

- Stop being driven; slow down

- Set a budget and stick to it

- Tell others what we want instead of making them guess

- Ask others what they mean instead of mind reading

- Stop exaggerating
- Take the initiative to be a friend instead of remaining passive
- Stop to reflect on and correct behavior
- Quit rationalizing or being defensive when wrong
- Acknowledge cravings, fears, shames, bitterness and hatred
- Grieve losses instead of denying them
- And much more

All of these responsibilities are processes, of course, so you can expect to encounter wins and losses. But dysfunctional patterns can be broken. Healthy patterns of responsible behavior can be developed.

*G*rief and responsibility. Both. Not one or the other.

Grief and responsibility. Both. Not one or the other. We need to grieve our losses in order to experience true comfort and healing. And we need to take specific steps to become responsible for our emotions and our behavior. We need the Lord to communicate His love and grace to us. We need Him to be our "very present help in time of trouble" (Psalms 46:1). Then we can share that comfort with others, as Paul did:

> Blessed be the God and Father of our Lord Jesus Christ,
> the Father of mercies and God of all comfort;
> Who comforts us in all our affliction so that we may be able
> to comfort those who are in any affliction with the comfort
> with which we ourselves are comforted by God (2
> Corinthians 1:3–4).

Paradoxically, many of us who have felt most ashamed of our behavior, who are most self-deprecating and full of self-hatred, have the hardest time taking responsibility for our sins. Perhaps they are so threatening that we are afraid to admit their stark reality. We continue to punish ourselves for them. And rather than experiencing true forgiveness, we maintain a painful penance. David describes the consequences of covering up sin:

> When I kept silent about my sin, my body wasted away
> Through my groaning all day long.
> For day and night Thy hand was heavy upon me;
> My vitality was drained away as with the fever heat of
> summer (Psalms 32:3–4).

Then he took responsibility for his sins and experienced forgiveness:

> I acknowledged my sin to Thee,
> And my iniquity I did not hide;
> I said, 'I will confess my transgressions to the Lord';
> And Thou didst forgive the guilt of my sin (Psalms 32:5).

We all have made wrong choices. We have hurt people. We have offended the Lord. We may justify and rationalize our sinful behavior by saying that we were very hurt—and we were. But if the healing process is to take place, we must become more objective and stronger, admitting that we have sinned—and still do—in many ways. With this admission, we learn to experience true forgiveness.

The secular recovery movement often communicates that people should be responsible, but primarily to themselves. They are encouraged to "Take care of yourself," and "Do something for yourself today." These admonitions are good to a point, but they are only part of the solution.

As we learn to grieve and to take responsibility for ourselves, we discover the wisdom, balance, and maturity to determine healthy relationships. And in doing so, we avoid the extremes of self-preoccupation on one side or the loss of identity and personhood on the other.

In the family of God, we are also encouraged to "bear our own load" (Galatians 6:5) and take care of our own needs. Yet we are also part of a community of believers who are called to honor God and to behave responsibly toward others. As we learn to grieve and to take responsibility for ourselves, we discover the wisdom, balance, and maturity to determine healthy relationships. And in doing so, we avoid the extremes of self-preoccupation on one side or the loss of identity and personhood on the other.

REFLECTION/DISCUSSION

1. Many of us have tried to "suck it up" and be responsible without grieving our losses. Why does this approach often lead to depression?

   But why do you think it often sounds like the right thing to do?

2. We can also get stuck in the mire of self-pity. What are some results (in yourself or your relationships) of prolonged self-pity?

3. In what ways is it more comfortable to be a victim than to be responsible?

4. Where are you on the responsibility-grief scale now? How do you know?

5. Describe what it means to "grieve." Which model of grief seems most accurate to you? Why?

6. In what ways is grief cathartic? In what ways is it drudging?

7. Why do most people think they are farther along in the grieving process than they actually are?

8. Review the list of responsibilities in this chapter. Which do you need to focus on at this point? Why? How will taking responsibility for these aspects of your life affect you?

9. Read Psalm 23. How does this psalm show how David experienced comfort and took responsibility?

[1] Elisabeth Kübler-Ross, *On Death and Dying* (New York: MacMillan Publishing, 1969).

[2] For more detail on these steps, see *Your Parents and You,* Robert S. McGee, Jim Craddock, and Pat Springle; or *Codependency: A Christian Perspective* 2d ed., Pat Springle (Houston and Dallas: Rapha Publishing/ Word, Inc., 1990).

[3] John W. James and Frank Cherry, *The Grief Recovery Handbook: A Step-by-Step Program for Moving Beyond Loss* (New York: Harper and Row, 1988), p. 10.

[4] Charlotte A. Greeson, Mary Hollingsworth, and Michael Washburn, *Grief Adjustment Guide: A Pathway Through Pain* (Sisters, OR: Questar Publishers, Inc., 1990), p. 68.

[5] Ibid.

11

◆

New Mirrors

—Pat Springle

W HEN I WAS IN HIGH SCHOOL (which at this point seems like it was just after Columbus landed), one of the most popular television shows was "The Twilight Zone." Rod Serling introduced each program in his deep, mysterious voice while strange, ethereal images flashed on the screen. I vividly remember one of these shows. (It's funny how you can remember some things you'd rather forget and forget some things you need to remember.)

A couple from another planet—Martians, no doubt—had been operated on by a team of plastic surgeons. Throughout the program, the couples' faces were bandaged, and strangely, the doctors' and nurses' faces were never shown either. All of the dialog revolved around the intense hope that the surgery would be successful and that the couple would look good and be accepted.

As the suspense grew (and the commercials passed), the time finally arrived for the bandages to be removed. Their faces were revealed. They looked into a mirror. They appeared to be two very attractive people. But then they both screamed. The man cried, "Oh, no! The surgery failed!"

The camera pulled back to reveal the doctors and nurses for the first time. Their faces were all what we would consider to be grotesquely distorted, yet it was obvious that they were quite "normal" for this planet. The "attractive" couple were the strange ones. Turning away from the couple in horror, a nurse anguished, "How horrible! I can't bear to look at them."

In the Twilight Zone, beauty was ugliness and ugliness was beauty. The perception of the onlookers was what made all the difference.

In much the same way, our perception is not always correct. It becomes distorted as we look at images of ourselves through the mirrors of our dysfunctional families. In the reflection of abusive or neglectful parents, we see ourselves as worthless and unlovable. These mirrors twisted the perceptions we have of ourselves, others, and God. When this happens, we need new mirrors.

The powerful combination of God's Word and God's people can change our lives as we increasingly learn to see ourselves in the mirrored reflection of truth, kindness, patience, and love.

Two mirrors to help us regain an accurate perception are the Scriptures and the family of God. Both help us learn to see more clearly. They help us avoid both the distorted reflections from our dysfunctional families and the Pollyanna, rose-colored outlook that everything is always wonderful. The powerful combination of God's Word and God's people can change our lives as we increasingly learn to see ourselves in the mirrored reflection of truth, kindness, patience, and love. Let's look at these features one at a time.

TRUTH

The anchor of our lives should not be our personal experience, but rather the truth of God's Word. The actual character of God is the goal of our search, not our previous perceptions of Him. Some of us read about the love of God, but feel guilty. We listen to talks about His comforting strength, but still feel oppressed. Our perceptions have been twisted. But others who have been on the recovery journey longer can help change these views by "speaking the truth in love" (Ephesians 4:15). They can help us discover the truth about God, about ourselves, and about every issue in our lives.

If we have read the Bible in the reflection of our distorted mirrors, we may not have been able to see the truth it proclaims. New friends can help us understand and apply its incisive and life-changing truths. The Bible can help us understand our deepest longings and motives. The writer of Hebrews wrote:

> The word of God is living and active and sharper than any two-edged sword, and piercing as far as the division of soul and spirit, of both joints and marrow, and able to judge the thoughts and intentions of the heart.
> And there is no creature hidden from His sight, but all things are open and laid bare to the eyes of Him with whom we have to do (Hebrews 4:12–13).

Scripture gives us insight into the entire process of perception, application, and true change in our lives. Paul reflected:

> All Scripture is inspired by God and profitable for teaching, for reproof, for correction, for training in righteousness; That the man of God may be adequate, equipped for every good work (2 Timothy 3:16–17).

We may fear the truth, afraid of being devastated by it and finding out that we are worse off than we thought. But a loving friend will tell us the truth with grace, and we will learn to appreciate the person's willingness to be honest with us. The wounds that may be inflicted by hearing the truth are like surgery to remove a tumor: it may hurt, but we know it's for our own good.

KINDNESS

The Scriptures also speak boldly and clearly of the kindness of God. Jesus was very busy with a heavy load of responsibility while He was on earth, yet He was kind to those who were outcasts in society. A leper told Him, "If you are willing, you can make me clean." Jesus responded in kindness, "I am willing," and healed him (Matthew 8:1–3). The disciples wanted to make little children leave Jesus alone, yet Jesus stopped to give them His full attention and to bless them (Mark 10:13–16).

Paul reminded the believers in Rome that "the kindness of God leads . . . to repentance" (Romans 2:4). Paul also explains that the ultimate purpose of God is to express His kindness to us for all eternity:

> [God] raised us up with Him, and seated us with Him in
> the heavenly places, in Christ Jesus,
> In order that in the ages to come He might show the
> surpassing riches of His grace in kindness toward us in
> Christ Jesus (Ephesians 2:6–7).

Over the past few years, I have been learning to appreciate not only God's kindness, but also the kindnesses of others expressed toward me. As we experience the genuine affection of other believers, we see that even their reproofs are acts of kindness, meant for our good. We should learn to echo David's invitation, "Let the righteous smite me in kindness" (Psalms 141:5).

PATIENCE

"Even though you blew it, that's okay. I still care about you."

Words that express patience soothe and encourage us. Two of my favorites are "even though" (as in, "Even though you blew it, that's okay. I still care about you"). Even though Thomas doubted . . . even though he wasn't around when Jesus first appeared to the disciples . . . even though he publicly expressed his doubts . . . Jesus was patient with him (John 20:19–29).

If I had been Jesus, I would have said, "Well, forget about him! If that's the way he feels after all I've done for him. . . ." But Jesus didn't respond that way. He made another appearance:

> He said to Thomas, "Reach here your finger, and see My
> hands; and reach here your hand, and put it into My side;
> and be not unbelieving, but believing.
> Thomas answered and said to Him, "My Lord and my
> God!" (John 20:27–28)

Several people have displayed that kind of patience with
me. They have consistently told me the truth with patience and
persistence, "even though" I didn't understand, or might have
reacted negatively toward them. I don't know where I would be
today without their help.

LOVE

Almost everybody has a favorite passage on the love of God.
Here is mine:

> See how great a love the Father has bestowed upon us,
> that we should be called children of God; and such we are.
> For this reason the world does not know us, because it did
> not know Him.
> Beloved, now we are children of God, and it has not
> appeared as yet what we shall be. We know that, when He
> appears, we shall be like Him, because we shall see Him
> just as He is (1 John 3:1–2).

"How great a love" . . . "lavished" . . . "children" . . . . These
words describe a rich and deep commitment of God toward you and
me. God's people, too, can communicate such a commitment toward
each other. David and Jonathan's strong commitment to each
other is vividly depicted in 1 Samuel. Jonathan's defense of David
brought on the wrath of his father, King Saul, and Saul even tried
to kill Jonathan for it (1 Sam. 20:32–33). Yet Jonathan remained
loyal to his friend.

When I was in college at the University of Georgia, I was
involved in a renewal movement. (We called it an "awakening.")
The Lord was at work changing lives—including mine! Hundreds
of people became believers and talked openly about their faith. But
my most vivid memories of that unique experience are of the loving
relationships I witnessed. It didn't matter how big the meetings

were or how many people went to the conferences. I became part of that movement because of love expressed through a million acts of sacrificial kindness toward friends and strangers alike. People like myself were drawn to that environment like a moth to a flame.

Today such relationships are rarer, but just as life-changing. As the people of God express the love of God, defenses are broken down and healing occurs. These powerful mirrors provide new perceptions which enable others to see themselves clearly.

Increasing exposure to accurate mirrors clarifies the previous distortions we have had about ourselves and/or our families. We need the give-and-take of meaningful interaction to focus our vision and see if our budding perceptions are accurate. Our perceptions are frequently mired to some degree in the bog of denial, and we need the help of others to enable us to get a clear picture of our need for healing and restoration.

Seeing Our Pain

The hurt we feel—or suppress—is usually a complicated morass of present wounds, past wounds, and established dysfunctional behavior patterns with their complicating consequences. Our healing process continues as we learn to identify the myriad sources of our pain and grieve each one.

Present wounds such as rejection, condemnation, being ignored or manipulated, failure, etc., are common occurrences—results of the Fall. But as painful as these wounds are, they are greatly compounded by wounds from the past. Repressed hurt and anger continue to build and fester, making us increasingly sensitive to freshly inflicted wounds. A tap on a healthy arm causes little pain, but the same tap on a broken, uncared for, inflamed arm creates shock waves of excruciating pain.

Both present and past wounds are further complicated by a lifestyle which prevents healing and promotes continued dysfunctional behavior. Addictions, rescuing, being driven to perform, passivity, depression, blaming, irresponsibility, over-responsibility, and a host of other behavior patterns are intended to help us block pain and gain acceptance. But in reality, they create more pain and block healthy development.

Another element that contributes to our pain is the reality

of living with the consequences of our lifestyles. Whether or not we understand our behavior patterns, we reap what we sow: strained relationships, bitterness, depression, debt, a bad reputation, inability to get or hold on to a job, and tangled webs of controlling and manipulative relationships.

But in the clear mirrors of the Scriptures and godly friends, we are able to slowly sort out the sources of our pain. The wounds can then be grieved and healed. We can experience forgiveness for the sins which have strained our relationships, and we can extend forgiveness to those who have wounded us. We can establish new patterns of living with proper responsibility, respect, and love, trusting only those who are trustworthy. And we can slowly learn to accept those consequences which cannot change and make right those which can.

EXPERIENCING OUR FEELINGS

Though some of us are histrionic by nature and others are more selectively passionate about causes or people, most of us are guilty of emotional explosions when the lid comes off our fear, hurt, or anger. The most common way we deal with our outbursts is by controlling our emotions through denial, repression, and suppression.

The Bible is about real people with real fears, real longing, real guilt, and real love. As we read their stories, we need to search not only for what they did, but also for how they felt.

Somehow, modern Christianity seems to have taken emotion out of faith. We have made Christ to appear staid and nonexpressive. We fail to comprehend the tenderness in His relationships with children, His gentleness in correcting Peter, or His anger as He proclaimed "woes" on the heartless religious leadership. We read facts and narratives, but we miss the discouragement, joy, hatred, despair, and contentment contained within them. The Bible is about real people with real fears, real longing, real guilt, and real love. As we read their stories, we need to search not only for what they did, but also for how they felt.

Obviously, one reason we fail to see the depth and breadth of emotions in the Bible is that we project our own stuffed feelings onto its characters. Their feelings are perceived as flat because *ours* are flat. In the environment of honest, growing relationships, however, we can learn to "own" our emotions.

Recently I met with a small group, and as we talked about the tendency to repress feelings, one woman lamented, "But I don't even know what my feelings are! How can I choose to feel them?

We gave her two suggestions: "First, several times a day for a month, write in a pocket journal how you feel. At first, you may record only confusion that you don't feel anything. Then you may get angry because you want to feel, but can't. You may also want to look at the 'Feelings Word List' on page 188 of *Close Enough to Care*.[1] It will help prod your ability to identify your feelings.

"Also talk to a friend about how you feel. Take the risk of sharing about your longings, fears, anger, hopes, and happiness. Your friend may ask, 'What were three emotions you had today?' so you can reflect on and discuss them. Reflecting on your emotions, 'owning' them, and telling someone else how you feel will help you grow in your ability to experience your true feelings."

The context of a group is a wonderful environment in which to learn to feel. In the early stages of overcoming repression, we often experience emotional spasms and paroxysms. These outbursts, fits, and starts may scare us—so much that we go back to repressing them. But as we see others grapple with repression and emotional confusion, we can identify. We understand them, so we understand ourselves: "I'm not the only one. He felt the same way when he started and he's doing better now. Maybe I can make it, too."

SEEING OUR CHOICES

Sarah told me, "I never even knew I had choices—because I didn't see any! I thought being manipulated, condemned, and then feeling guilty because I couldn't do enough to make my husband happy was the only way to live. Love ... respect ... choices ... no, I only knew one way to live."

Our interaction with the Scriptures and close friends or a support group can help us see that we have real choices—hard choices sometimes, but choices nonetheless. One man related in his group, "I thought it was up to me to make people happy—not just a few people, everybody! I tried for a while, but wrecked my marriage, my job, and my health . . . so I gave up. I felt hopeless. I didn't really want to come to this group, but I was desperate. In the last six months, I've learned that I have choices. Sometimes I'm too scared to make the right one, but at least I know that I have them! I'm learning to choose whom to trust and whom I can't trust, what I'm responsible for and what I'm not, what is true and what is denial and deception. I feel like a kid with a new, complicated toy. I'm not sure how to put it together yet, but I'm making progress."

> . . . *The Bible reflects the need for honesty, confession, and renewal. Instead of being easily manipulated, mature people consider their options, motives, and the consequences of their choices.*

The clarity of choices is a direct result of better vision from our new mirrors. Instead of denial, the Bible reflects the need for honesty, confession, and renewal. Instead of being easily manipulated, mature people consider their options, motives, and the consequences of their choices. A proverb relates the difference between *reacting* (without thinking) and *responding* in wisdom: "A wicked man shows a bold face, but as for the upright, he makes his way sure" (Proverbs 21:29).

Those who impulsively react to people and situations show "a bold face." They demand and then react in anger when their demands aren't met. But the "upright" person reflects on his choices before he responds. He "makes his way sure."

Instead of allowing ourselves to be driven to perform, Jesus encourages us to discover peace and establish proper priorities. The classic story of Mary and Martha is one example:

> Now as they were traveling along, He entered a certain village; and a woman named Martha welcomed Him into her home.

And she had a sister called Mary, who moreover was
listening to the Lord's word, seated at His feet.
But Martha was distracted with all her preparations; and
she came up to Him, and said, "Lord, do You not care that
my sister has left me to do all the serving alone?
Then tell her to help me."
But the Lord answered and said to her, "Martha, Martha,
you are worried and bothered about so many things;
But only a few things are necessary, really only one, for
Mary has chosen the good part, which shall not be taken
away from her" (Luke 10:38–42).

SEEING OUR GROWTH

"I must be reading the Bible with new eyes," a lady said
excitedly. "I'm seeing things I've never seen before, like grace, love,
and peace. Same passages . . . new eyes, I guess." Later she told me,
"Since I've been involved in my support group, I've felt really
discouraged sometimes. I felt like I wasn't making any progress at
all—going backward, if anything. But as I keep at it, and as others
in the group tell me they see specific changes and new perceptions,
I realize that I *am* growing!"

Growth may be slow. In fact, the early stages do seem to
take us backward. But our new mirrors help us maintain a clear
picture of growth—not instantaneous black-to-white change, but
slow and steady progress.

We have talked about how the Scriptures and godly people
provide new mirrors for us. Our responsibility is to find a nurturing
environment and respond with courage as we discover the new
choices we have. Yet our ability to comprehend and change is
affected by two other essential ingredients in the healing process:
the Holy Spirit and time.

Lasting growth is not achieved by self-effort; it comes as the
Spirit of God provides wisdom, strength, and true change. Sometimes this growth may come quickly; other times it will be painfully
slow. It's not unlike the experience of a farmer who sees rapid
progress in his crop at certain points of its development, but more
frequently endures long and slow waiting periods prior to harvest.
The healing process hinges on both our endeavors to take responsibility for ourselves and God's enablement to help us do so. Then,
over time, we will have no reason to be disappointed with the
reflection we see in our new mirrors.

REFLECTION/DISCUSSION

1. The powerful combination of the Scriptures and the functioning family of God can help us develop new perceptions and lifestyles. Paraphrase the following passages which describe aspects of these "new mirrors":

    *   Truth—Hebrews 4:12–13

    *   Kindness—1 Thessalonians 5:14

    *   Love—Ephesians 4:13–16

2. Our "new mirrors" also help us see clearly enough so we can repair the damage done by distortions of the past. How do these new relationships help you:

    *   see the dysfunction in your family and yourself?

    *   have the courage to feel repressed emotions?

- see that you have more choices than you ever saw before?

- see your steps of growth and healing?

[1] Pat Springle, *Close Enough to Care* by (Houston and Dallas: TX, Rapha Publishing/Word, Inc., 1990).

12

◆

Trust
and
Love

—*Pat Springle*

We all have an instinctive longing for "love." But to be truthful, many of us don't have the foggiest notion what it really is.

Bill had been in a support group for almost a year when he told other group members, "I'm kind of confused. I've been getting stronger, setting limits, seeing choices, taking responsibility for my behavior, and all that. But lately it seems that I don't know what love is. I used to know—at least I thought I did. I really thought I had 'close relationships' in the past, but now I realize I was just manipulating those people to get them to act like they cared. I didn't give them the choice to care about me. Now I feel really empty . . . and lonely."

Others see the situation from a different angle. Instead of finding substitutes for love, they give up. Instead of filling their lives with relationships, they withdraw. It's not that they think they know what love is when they actually don't. Rather, they are only too aware that they are alone, empty, and without hope of loving or being loved.

As we get farther along in the emotional healing process and develop clearer perception, we are able to see the contrasts between love and its counterfeits. One group was asked, "How do people in dysfunctional families communicate?" The predictable answers included a wide array of verbal and nonverbal communications (yelling, withdrawal, glaring, condemning, praising in order to manipulate, silence for weeks or months, demanding, rolling eyes, smothering with instructions, etc.). Then the leader wrote three words on the blackboard: "Love, Trust, Respect." The group breathed an almost audible sigh. It was as if they, as one person, realized the difference between the oppression of abuse and neglect, and the nurturing of love, trust, and respect. It is like the difference between watering and fertilizing a plant and crushing it with a boot or letting it wilt and die from lack of water.

Psychologist Erik Erikson describes trust as the earliest stage in a person's emotional development.[1] Trust is developed if the child feels safe and protected, confident and secure. Then he can assimilate his parents' affection and receive their love.

Though loving adult relationships aren't formed until much later in adolescence when the child's identity is more developed, the foundation of trust is necessary for the development of love. It is not too much to say, then, that in any relationship, trust is the basis of love and intimacy.

If a family is dysfunctional (neglectful, smothering, attacking, etc.), the child will feel threatened and unsafe. A child may acutely realize that his environment is unstable and that his parents and siblings are untrustworthy, but they are the only world he knows. His basic choices are to either trust nobody or to trust everybody, including those who are untrustworthy.

Sandra was from a divorced home. Her father left when she was about seven, so her mother had to go to work to provide for Sandra and her brother, Paul. Consequently, Sandra's earliest memories were of bitterness, yelling, door slamming, withdrawal, and other tensions between her parents. She concluded that she couldn't trust anybody, and she became fiercely independent. Her brother reached the opposite conclusion. He blindly trusted his mother and clung to the belief that his father was trustworthy, too.

Both Sandra and Paul experienced "splitting"—developing a perception of life as "black or white." They came to see people as "for them or against them," as "friends or enemies," as "good or bad." Sandra avoided intimacy, afraid of being hurt again. But her brother's craving for intimacy led him to trust the wrong people, giving himself blindly in hopes that they would meet his needs. Sandra tried to dominate people by her wit and rapier tongue. Paul tried to control people by doing whatever made them happy.

In his late twenties, however, Paul's blind trust was shattered. Through a series of events—a broken engagement, a strained relationship with his boss, and the constant nagging of his mother—he finally broke. His blind trust disintegrated and his perception of others went from white to black. He trusted no one, and even felt that God had abandoned him. "I used to feel so close to God and to people," Paul said with a voice of both sadness and anger. "But they let me down."

Without the strong foundation of trust, both Sandra and Paul had become confused about love. They redefined it to fit their experience.

| We confuse: | PITY WORRY DOMINATION NEED RESCUING CORRECTION | with LOVE. |

CONFUSION ABOUT LOVE

In response to the blindness and poor modeling of our families, many of us define love, describe love, and act out "love" in ways that are distorted and painful. We confuse love with a host of other feelings and actions. In *Close Enough to Care*, several distortions are listed, which are summarized below.[2]

We confuse *pity* with love. We sometimes think that feeling sorry for someone is the same as loving them. This distorted love is expressed in statements such as, "It's just terrible! I wish that hadn't happened to you. You must be suffering so much." Empathy, the identification with another person, *is* a part of love. But pity is not the same as empathy, and it certainly isn't the same as genuine love.

We confuse *worry* with love. "I am just worried *sick* about you! I stayed up all night worrying about you!" Comments like these are designed to manipulate others through guilt, not communicate value and clear consequences to behavior.

We confuse *domination* with love. This tendency might be expressed by an immature adolescent as, "I know my Dad loves me because he does everything for me, and tells me what to do in every situation." But as we get older and more mature, our response to domination might be more like the wife who was not so positive: "My husband won't let me go anywhere without him. He controls even the people I talk to on the phone! He says he does this to protect me because he loves me."

We confuse *need* with love. "You're the only one who really understands me. I don't know what I'd do without you. I need you so much!" People frequently use statements like these to control others, not out of respect and love. The intense emotion and the closeness felt may seem like love, but it is enmeshment.

We confuse *rescuing* with love. Love doesn't keep people dependent on us to fix their problems and make them happy. That tendency comes from our own need for value, not genuine love and respect. We tell our children, "I'll help you," and, "Wait, let me do that for you." But as they grow, we need to gradually let them take more responsibility for their own choices—to let them fail and struggle and learn to cope with real life.

We confuse *correction* with love. "I'm telling you this for your own good." That statement is then followed by a barrage of orders to correct a person's behavior. Correction can certainly be one part of a healthy, loving relationship that involves trust and "speaking the truth in love" (Ephesians 4:15). But if correction becomes the primary foundation, the relationship is not likely to be a truly loving one.

God created us to be relational beings. We need to give and receive love. If these needs are not met, a vortex (or "black hole," as one man called it) develops. We discover we have a craving for love. We thirst for it, and in our desperation we may try to quench that thirst with the emotional equivalent of sand, poison, or ashes.

Ultimately, God is the benchmark of real love, and the fountain from which we can quench our thirst. Jesus made reference to this as he spoke to the crowd on a feast day in Jerusalem:

> Now on the last day, the great day of the feast, Jesus stood and cried out, saying, "If any man is thirsty, let him come to Me and drink.
> He who believes in Me, as the Scripture said, 'From his innermost being shall flow rivers of living water.'"
> But this He spoke of the Spirit, whom those who believed in Him were to receive; for the Spirit was not yet given, because Jesus was not yet glorified (John 7:37–39).

God is the source of love, and His people are to act as His arms and hands to help communicate His love to others. The body of Christ, the people who have experienced His love and grace, can comfort those who are afraid, soothe and encourage those who are ashamed, model forgiveness and repentance to those who are consumed with hatred, and satisfy the needs of those who crave.

GRIEF AND GROWTH

People in the healing process usually go through many cycles of identifying wounds, grieving losses, and taking responsibility for the past, present, and future. At first, the recognition of wounds usually triggers much anger and sadness. As the process continues, however, the person develops a better understanding of the wound and how he has been affected by the absence of nurturing and affection.

In these later stages of the growth process, more of the intricacies of trust, love, and control become evident. The person is no longer shocked to discover that the wound is deeper than he thought. He sees patterns in his relationships more clearly. And in seeing these patterns, he realizes he has choices.

Responsibility and choices go hand in hand. The Lord begins to show us the way out of the deep pit of denial, and it is up to us to respond. We're afraid, but we take the first steps of talking to someone about our hurt and anger. If our trust isn't violated by someone who breaks confidentiality or gives us quick answers, we learn to risk a little more and become more honest. We choose to talk more, feel more, and keep growing.

At each stage of the process we take responsibility for our growth, for our sins, and for new characteristics in relationships. Though we could divide our responsibilities any number of ways, let's examine four basic groupings.

Trust—We should find nurturing and healing relationships, yet we should always remember that only God is completely trustworthy. The people who care about us are only human. They may unintentionally let us down, but usually they won't. Initially, the risk of being honest and vulnerable with other people may be frightening. And at every stage, we may be threatened by going deeper and being more honest as new skeletons are found in other closets. Yet as our trust grows, our capacity for love and intimacy grows as well.

Forgiveness—We may be victims of heinous abuses, and we need to fully grieve those wounds. But we also need to take responsibility to forgive and ask to be forgiven. Harboring resentment and desiring revenge is destructive, while forgiveness releases the offender from the debt and us from the hell of hatred. Whether or not they mean to, unforgiving victims inflict wounds on those around them. Taking responsibility for our sins on a continuing basis is a necessary step toward health and a life which honors God.

Limits—We may have trusted and loved those who were untrustworthy or who victimized us. We may have developed a pattern of trusting everyone or no one. But we can learn to love and respect other people, and to and value their identity, without giving up our own sense of value. We are responsible to set limits which encourage healthy communication yet maintain individual integrity.

New patterns in relationships—As we experience love and begin to set limits, we see the need to replace old patterns of communication (nagging, cursing, controlling, fixing, abandoning, etc.) with new patterns (listening, valuing the person, honesty, and integrity). These new patterns won't develop automatically. They are the product of all we have mentioned: grieving wounds and replacing defense mechanisms with a growing sense of self-esteem and genuine love and respect for others.

LOVE AND IDENTITY

One of the primary components in the ability to give and receive love is a sense of identity. Since expressing love requires a sharing of identities, many of us are at a distinct disadvantage. When people are well into the healing process, when their facade of defense mechanisms is being dismantled, a common comment is, "I don't even know who I am any more. I'm just now finding out that I'm not who I thought I was. I've played so many games and worn so many masks. I wonder who I am?"

We are still vulnerable and needy, but we have reached the point of taking the risk to trust someone who can nurture and encourage us.

Many of us perceive this condition as tragic. We feel hopeless and lonely. But this realization is a critical juncture in the healing process and a platform for real progress. Our defenses have been proven deficient. Our relationships, based on false identity, have been shallow. We are still vulnerable and needy, but we have reached the point of taking the risk to trust someone who can nurture and encourage us. We are at a point, too, of crying out to the Lord in honesty about our needs.

During this period, the sense of love and value we receive provides fertile soil in which to grow, and we begin to develop a new identity. The demolition of the facade allows the construction of a new sense of value based on the unconditional love of God instead of our own abilities to block pain, succeed, and please people.

Our growing capacity to receive love is soon followed by a growing capacity to give love. Manipulation, control, and withdrawal are gradually replaced by honesty, love, and respect. We are at last honest enough to admit that our needs are even greater than we ever imagined. We had repressed our wants so long because we were afraid of them, but now we are stronger and more comfortable with our needs. They don't threaten us like before.

We also come to realize that God is trustworthy. Perhaps we had felt that if He met our every need, then He could be trusted.

If He didn't, we concluded that either something was wrong with us, or that God was no longer trustworthy. We didn't understand "trust." We wanted to control God. We wanted Him to be safe.

But God is not trustworthy because He can be controlled. He is trustworthy because He is infinitely loving, kind, strong, good, and wise. In C.S. Lewis' classic children's series, *The Chronicles of Narnia*, two children, Susan and Lucy, talk to Mrs. Beaver about the great lion, Aslan (symbolic of Jesus). The children are trying to determine if Aslan is trustworthy:

> "Ooh," said Susan, "I thought he was a man. Is he—quite safe? I shall feel rather nervous about meeting a lion."
> "That you will, dearie, and no mistake," said Mrs. Beaver, "if there's anyone who can appear before Aslan without their knees knocking, they're either braver than most or else just silly."
> "Then he isn't safe?" said Lucy.
> "Safe?" said Mr. Beaver, "Don't you hear what Mrs. Beaver tells you? Who said anything about safe? 'Course he isn't safe. But he's good. He's the king, I tell you."[3]

God is not safe, but He is good. He is not controllable, but He is trustworthy.

God is not safe, but He is good. He is not controllable, but He is trustworthy. Because He *is* trustworthy, we can entrust ourselves to Him, be honest with Him, learn to be loved by Him, and love Him in return.

Trust is developed, defenses are worn away, and we develop a new identity. Our thirst for love becomes satisfied by God's living water. And while our fallen natures prevent the fullest satisfaction until we see Him face to face, for those of us who have craved love without our thirst being quenched, the genuine satisfaction we experience is enough for now.

REFLECTION/DISCUSSION

1. How are trust and love related? Can there be trust without love? Love without trust?

2. If we do not learn to be perceptive in our trust (that is, learn to trust those who are trustworthy), then we tend to either trust people blindly or not trust anyone at all. Trusting blindly assumes that most people are good, kind, and fair. Lack of trust cynically assumes that people are usually selfish, mean, and unfair. Perceptive trust realizes that people are neither "black" nor "white," but varying shades of "gray." List some characteristics of each of the following kinds of trust and the corresponding results.

   BLIND TRUST
   Characteristics:

   Results:

   LACK OF TRUST
   Characteristics:

   Results:

   PERCEPTIVE TRUST
   Characteristics:

   Results:

   Is blind trust better or worse than a lack of trust? Why?

Which kinds of trust characterize your life? Why?

3. How is perceptive trust developed?

4. Which of the "confusions about love" have been true of you? How has confusion affected you and your relationships?

5. Describe how your love is growing as you progress in the areas of:

Trust

Forgiveness

Limits

New patterns in relationships

6. Trust is the foundation of every relationship, including your relationship with God. Paraphrase the following passages:

Romans 5:1

Galatians 5:6

Ephesians 2:8–10

Colossians 1:3–5

Hebrews 11:6

[1] Erikson, Eric. *Identity: Youth and Crisis.* New York: Norton, 1968.

[2] Springle, Pat. *Close Enough to Care.* Houston and Dallas: Rapha Publishing/Word, Inc., 1990.

[3] Lewis, C.S. *The Lion, The Witch and the Wardrobe.* New York: Macmillan, 1950, pp. 75–76.

13

◆

Trust
and
Control

—*Robert S. McGee*

Joanne had been in the healing process for over a year. She was making considerable progress, though she still experienced deep feelings of shame quite frequently. As a child she had been smothered with attention and tightly controlled by her single mother, and as an adult she herself had become a very controlling mother of her two young sons.

Joanne had experienced difficulty seeing how tightly she controlled her children. "I just want the best for them," she would say, "and the Lord knows how little boys need a mother's guidance!" Joanne's mother had made her decisions for her, and now Joanne was making all her sons' decisions for them.

We began to talk about trust, and slowly "the lights began to come on." We talked about how her mother had not provided a safe environment, and how Joanne had been afraid to do anything except what her mother wanted. After several such conversations, Joanne blurted out, "I guess I couldn't trust anybody, so I had to control them to protect myself."

"Yes," I answered, "you controlled them by doing what they—especially your mother—wanted."

Joanne concluded, "I controlled her by pleasing her, and she controlled me with the threat of disapproval. . . . I never saw that before."

Trying to control people through methods such as fear, threats, withdrawal, or attacks shows a lack of respect for their identity and separateness. In the previous chapter, we saw how trust is the foundation of love. Now we will examine how trust is also instrumental in developing a healthy sense of identity so that we don't fall into one of two extremes: being an *island* (without meaningful relationships) or a *puppet* (without a healthy sense of independence).

Without a safe environment, we cannot trust. Without trust, we cannot develop the capacity to give and receive love. Without a healthy sense of being loved by—or bonded to—other people, we are quite susceptible to problems with separateness. We either withdraw and become islands to avoid pain, or we become puppets who do whatever anyone wants.

Controlling others—Many psychologists identify roles that people play in attempts to control others in their families:

"Mascots" tell jokes during tense interactions to relieve pressure.
"Heroes" try to be the best at sports, work, school, housekeeping, or some other area. They want to prove their worth and control how other people treat them, always craving praise.
"Scapegoats" control others by misbehaving. If it takes yelling, cursing, or whatever, to get people to talk to you, it's still better than silence.
"Enablers" are classic controllers. By fixing others' problems, they keep those people dependent on them. Enablers give advice when it isn't requested. They use a variety of methods to control people with the threat of rejection. Praise is meted out sparsely to reward and reinforce "good" (controllable) behavior.
The **"lost child"** controls others quite differently. He is quiet and withdrawn to keep people from hurting him. Since communication involves the risk of additional pain, it is avoided. Alcoholics, addicts, and people with other severely dysfunctional behaviors also control others through self-pity, rage, needing to be rescued, and other methods.

These roles tend to be played out each of the person's relationships, not just within the family. A person who "enables" her alcoholic husband, for example, usually seeks out other people who need her help as well. They let her control them just as her husband does. These people may resent being controlled, but that liability is outweighed by the perceived benefits of the help received. And the cycle continues.

Being controlled—Some of us are well aware of how we use sarcasm, praise, neglect, etc., to control others, but we completely miss how we allow ourselves to be controlled by others. This may become apparent only after we have been in the healing process for a while.

Our control of others can be similar to or quite different from the way we have been controlled. For instance, one man who had been rigidly controlled by a harsh, demanding mother treated his wife and children the same way. But a lady with a similar background tried to win the affection of her family by being very lenient and affirming. "I also tried to control people at work in the same way," she told me. "I guess I thought that if I gave them lots of freedom, they would give me the affirmation I wanted. I wanted to be loved so badly. . . . I just wanted them to like me, so I gave them what they wanted."

Unmet needs for love and safety open the door to manipulation and unhealthy control by others. In dysfunctional families, children intuitively learn what it takes to avoid pain and get emotional strokes. They gravitate toward one of two extremes—either withdrawing to avoid pain, or thinking, feeling, saying, and doing whatever will please others. They control others even while they are being controlled.

IDENTITY AND SELF-CONTROL

Harry sat in my office and expressed his frustration at being oppressed by his father. "I'm 45 years old. I live 1500 miles from my Dad. I would think that I'd be free from his control, but I'm not. Whenever I try to do something at work, tapes of his voice are replayed in my mind telling me, *You're gonna mess up! You're a failure! Don't even bother to try!*" Harry reflected for a few seconds and then said, "I guess he still has the power to ruin my life, and I can't do anything about it."

Harry's sense of shame, self-hatred, and hopelessness is a common phenomenon, but he was wrong. Something *can* be done about it. Like him, we may have grown up in unsafe families where we felt the need to control and be controlled, and where we gave up the power to be ourselves and make our own decisions. But we can take that power back and exercise it appropriately.

We need to understand power from a biblical perspective. Power is not sin. But like many other things, power can be used selfishly or harmfully, in which cases it becomes sinful. If we use power to manipulate others, to control their behavior, then such use is wrong. Similarly, if power is used to control us, it is sinful. But power can be a resource for tremendous good, and God is the source of power which we should use to build and strengthen.

For example, Paul prayed for the believers at Ephesus, that they would "be strengthened with power through [God's] Spirit in the inner man" (Ephesians 3:16). And he reminded Timothy: "God has not given us a spirit of timidity, but of power and love and discipline" (2 Timothy 1:7).

Some of us believe that self-control requires suppressing our emotions. We tell ourselves, *Keep 'em under control.* However, self-control is not repression; it is the ability to make good choices instead of letting people or situations determine our responses. In a list of characteristics that should be reflected in the Christian life, Paul lists self-control as one evidence of God's Spirit in the life of believers:

> The fruit of the Spirit is love, joy, peace, patience, kindness,
> goodness, faithfulness, gentleness, self-control; against
> such things there is no law (Galatians 5:22–23).

Personal power and self-control are not ungodly attributes. In fact, God provides these things to people who are willing to use them constructively instead of in a manipulative manner. In our "black-or-white" mind-sets, some of us have seen others as all-powerful, but ourselves as hopelessly weak. We feel guilty when we consider ourselves to be anything other than puppets or islands. Our identity is based on the inability to make our own decisions. We see ourselves, like Harry, as hopelessly oppressed, easily manipulated, forever doomed. We may resent the power that oppresses us, but we feel too selfish and guilty to think of exercising any authority ourselves.

Or perhaps we see ourselves quite differently. Our ability to wield power over others has proven so successful that we assume it is up to us to determine others' behaviors and feelings. As a "benevolent dictator," we either bully or rescue those who are weak. And if they dare stand up to us, we condemn them for their stupidity and power grabbing. And all the while we are blind to our own thirst for control over others.

Some people remain primarily in either the "weakling" or "dictator" mode in relationships, but many of us vacillate between the two. In fact, a large percentage of people are relatively servile to people in authority over them, but powerful and controlling of those in inferior positions.

Martha, for instance, quietly acquiesced to her demanding husband, but then she expected the same kind of unquestioning obedience from her children. She felt "one-up" on her children and "one-down" in relation to her spouse. The nature of the parent/child relationship wasn't entirely responsible for Martha's behavior. She also carried out this pecking order approach in her relationships with friends. She allowed some to dominate her, while she tried to dominate others.

We are able to grieve the wounds of the past, to untangle the snarled web of hurt, control, and deception, and to begin to take responsibility. We gradually develop a new identity.

However, the establishment of new, safe relationships changes the way we relate to others. We are able to grieve the wounds of the past, to untangle the snarled web of hurt, control, and deception, and to begin to take responsibility. We gradually develop a new identity. Growing confidence in trustworthy people and a trustworthy God enables us to relax, to let defenses down, to be strengthened and encouraged, and to learn to be the people God wants us to be.

Though the healing process includes focusing on our wounds and sorting out our responsibilities, establishing a new identity is not self-focused narcissism. We must closely examine ourselves to become freed from oppressive, empty self-preoccupation and morbid introspection. Only then can we experience depth in relationships and freedom in our choices.

Susan described her growing sense of identity and self-control this way: "As I continue in my own healing process, I can feel, I can see, and I can choose." She explained what she meant.

> *I can feel.* Instead of stuffing my feelings and exploding later, I am much more in touch with my fears, anger, and hurt. Being honest about these painful feelings also enables me to experience the positive ones a lot more, like love, and peace, and happiness.

> *I can see.* The more I grow and the stronger I get, the less I am threatened by reality. Sometimes it hurts; sometimes I like it. But I'm not nearly as threatened by it as I used to be. Life is no longer so grandiose or awful—you know, black-or-white. There's a lot more gray, which means that life is more complex—not so simple and clear—but still not as threatening.

> *I can choose.* I can set limits. I can say yes, and I can say no. People and events used to control me, and I bounced from one reaction to another. Now I'm learning to make my own choices in relationships, values, schedules, and everything else. Sometimes I make mistakes, but they're *my* mistakes. Nobody made me do them. I am responsible. I can't blame anybody.

I asked Susan how her development was affecting her relationships, and especially her compulsion to control others. She said:

> The more my own sense of strength and identity is developed, the more I can let others be themselves, too. I don't feel like I have to *make* them agree with me or do what I want them to.

I can let them feel without fixing them or condemning them for "being out of control."

I can let them see reality and listen, you know, value what they say instead of imposing what *I* think on them.

And I can let them choose what they want and how they act. I can respect their individuality without condemning and controlling. If they need help, they can ask for it—what a novel idea for a rescuer!

To someone who is an island or a puppet, a strong sense of identity may seem threatening because the person fears it will lead to loneliness. But the reverse is true. A sense of identity allows us to be ourselves instead of playing games and erecting facades to hide behind. The process of taking down these facades may require periods of loneliness, but sooner or later real trust is developed. We begin to experience intimacy with a range of emotions based on genuine honesty and love: fear, anger, hurt, happiness, and joy.

CONTROL AND GOD

If we tend to try to control people, then we probably try to control God as well.

It is silly to assume that we can play the intricate game of "Control and Being Controlled" with all the people in our lives and yet have an untainted, pure relationship with God. If we tend to try to control people, then we probably try to control God as well. One man told me:

All my life I equated trust with control. I would only trust what—or who—I could control. If someone resisted my attempts to control him, then I concluded that this person was against me. When I became a Christian, I read in the Bible that God was trustworthy. All my new Christian friends said He was, too, and for a year or so everything went well: He answered my prayers; I felt good about Him. I trusted Him—at least I thought I trusted Him. But after a year or so, my life began to unravel. My wife and I had big problems, my boss was upset with me, and my parents told me I wasn't doing enough for them. I prayed, but nothing got better. After a while, I got depressed. I concluded that God wasn't trustworthy at all.

If we mistake control for trust in our relationships with God, we will be deeply disappointed sooner or later. God is far above our petty devices to control others, and it is precisely because He is both great *and* good that He is trustworthy. He will not allow us to assume that we can control Him. That faulty notion is harmful to us and dishonoring to Him. Our equation of trust and control must be changed—often painfully so—in order to learn to trust Him for who He is, not because we want Him to perform to suit our whims.

*T*he goodness and greatness of God is the foundation of our trust.

The goodness and greatness of God is the foundation of our trust. He invites us to experience His love and grace, and the prophet Isaiah encourages us to "Seek the Lord while He may be found; call upon Him while He is near" (Isaiah 55:6).

The omnipotent, omnipresent God is near. He is personable and genuinely loving . . . but He is also uncontrollable and inscrutable. Isaiah quotes the Lord:

"For My thoughts are not your thoughts, neither are your ways My ways," declares the Lord. "For as the heavens are higher than the earth, so are My ways higher than your ways, and My thoughts than your thoughts" (Isaiah 55:8–9).

In the process of developing trust and accepting our own identity, we realize that we may have controlled people, but we have never controlled God. A major step in our growth occurs when we begin to recognize and accept the fact that God is both good and great. We can't control Him, but we can trust Him.

REFLECTION/DISCUSSION

1. Elaborate on the statement, "If you cannot trust, you have to control."

2. Why is that statement true or not true for you?

3. How can you stop being controlled by others (without becoming obnoxious)?

4. How can you stop controlling others (and have a real relationship based on trust and love)?

5. In what ways is personal power a good and godly thing? In what ways can it be corrupted?

6. What are some ways you have tried to control God? What were some of the results?

7. Read Isaiah 40:27–31; 55:8–9. What do these passages say about:

   • Your ability to control God?

   • His power to control?

   • His wisdom?

14

◆

Progressive
Forgiveness

—Robert S. McGee

Forgiveness—releasing someone from a debt—is a central issue in life. When someone hurts us, a debt is incurred. Our sense of justice cries out, *He owes me!* Love and justice are the cornerstones of emotional stability. Writing about a child's innate sense of love and justice, author and theologian John Stott says:

> Justice without mercy is too strict, and mercy without justice too lenient . . . children know this instinctively. . . . The two most poignant cries of a child are "Nobody loves me" and "It isn't fair." Their sense of love and justice comes from God, who made them in His image, and who revealed Himself as holy love at the cross.[1]

Forgiveness doesn't come naturally. It seems awkward, at best; to some it seems absurd. In his article about forgiveness, "An Unnatural Act," Philip Yancey observes that all the laws of nature and economics are based on attitudes of eat or be eaten and take what you can get.[2] But he outlines three compelling motivations to go against the grain and forgive the offender. These reasons are "breaking the cycle of blame and pain," "loosening the stronghold of guilt on us and others," and "helping us understand that we are just like others—all of us need forgiveness."

The cleansing refreshment of genuine forgiveness is attractive, but sadly alien to many of us.

Two Errors

Christians (and nonbelievers alike) tend to make one of two errors: They either forgive too quickly or not at all.

Christians (and nonbelievers alike) tend to make one of two errors: They either forgive too quickly or not at all. Many conscientious Christians can quote Scripture about forgiveness. We know we *should* forgive—we feel terribly ashamed when we don't! So we go through the motions of doing it. But something's wrong. When we talk about the wounds in our lives, we inevitably talk about a parent or a spouse who has hurt us deeply. Inevitably, the response is like that of a pastor I talked with. When I mentioned a childhood problem he had endured because of his father, he interrupted me.

". . . but I've already forgiven him for that!" the pastor insisted, although he had ceased to function normally because of his repressed anger toward his father. These turbulent, unexpressed feelings had pushed him into clinical depression.

"Do you think there may be some hurts you haven't grieved about yet?" I asked.

He looked at me resentfully. "I told you. I've already forgiven him!"

Forgiveness is the release from a debt—the *whole* debt, not just part of it. Devout, well-intentioned Christians sometimes forgive as soon as they become aware of pain; but often, their compulsion to forgive quickly short circuits the process of grieving the real wound and forgiving the real offense.

Incomplete forgiveness produces repressed hurt and anger, but it also produces considerable confusion. "After all," the injured person insists, "I have done all I know to do. I forgave, didn't I?" So why do the feelings of hurt and anger continue? Then hopelessness is added to the problems of compulsive forgiving, hurt, anger, and confusion.

As the pastor mentioned earlier began to understand his incomplete forgiveness of his father, his defensive resentment slowly faded. "So that's why I'm still depressed," he said. "I *thought* I had forgiven, but . . . yeah, I'm hurting a lot more than I care to admit. I'm scared of it. And I'm so embarrassed! After all, I'm a pastor! I feel like I'm not *supposed* to be depressed."

On the other end of the spectrum are those who refuse to forgive at all. "Never!" one woman screamed. "I'll never forgive him for what he did to me!" The woman had been wounded by her verbally abusive husband, but her deepest wounds were caused by his physical abuse of their children. "And what he did to Billy and Lee Ann . . . Only an animal would treat children that way!"

Both incomplete forgiveness and no forgiveness lead to more bitterness. People who hold onto their bitterness usually find that the deep, festering wounds of the past are compounded by daily interaction with other people. Bitter people look for faults to blame, not love to nurture.

EXPERIENCING FORGIVENESS

Our ability to forgive is inextricably linked with our ability to receive forgiveness for ourselves. To put it another way, we will be unable to truly forgive others for their sins toward us if we don't experience forgiveness for our sins toward God and others.

This realization is a turning point. Many of us have repressed our hurt for years. We've been afraid of the rage we've glimpsed from time to time. We may have sensed the overwhelming emptiness and hopelessness lurking in the recesses of our hearts. We have been wounded. We have been wronged. We are victims.

Our "victim mentality" can become so pervasive that we don't assume responsibility for our own sinful behavior. We are victims, but we are also victimizers. For example, in a heated exchange between spouses during a counseling session, the wife continuously blamed the husband for the couple's problems. I waited for a lull in the fight, then asked, "Cindy, you have listed things James has done wrong . . . things he is responsible for. What are some things *you* have done wrong in the relationship?"

She looked stunned, then angry, "Why ask *me* a question like that? *He's* the one who hurt *me*! I haven't done anything *close* to what he's done to me!"

This kind of blame-shifting is black or white, all or nothing. Cindy's bitterness continued to fester because she was unwilling to admit that she had been wrong, too. According to her, all of their problems were her husband's fault. To be sure, some of them were! But forgiveness, reconciliation, intimacy, respect, and even communication were blocked because Cindy was unwilling to be honest about her own sins in the relationship.

Another marital conversation started out in a similar way with both partners blaming each other and defending themselves. But after a while, the husband said, "I blew it. I was wrong when I. . . ." His admission of fault and responsibility didn't solve all their problems right away, but it did open the door so that solutions could be found.

While some of us try to bury our sinfulness by blaming others, others go to the opposite extreme. We assume that *everything* is our fault, but when we take the first steps in the healing process and become aware of the magnitude of the hurt and anger in our lives, we often flip-flop, assigning all the blame to the offenders. Wise friends and counselors can help us sort out what is *our* responsibility and what is *others'* responsibility, what we need to confess and what we need to grieve.

Confessing sins toward God and others takes courage, but it frees us from the cycles of repression and blame. This is not just a modern-day experience. King David long ago described his silence and unwillingness to take responsibility for his sin in terms that indicate that his silence led to depression:

> When I kept silent about my sin, my body wasted away through my groaning all day long.
> For day and night Thy hand was heavy upon me; my vitality was drained away as with the fever heat of summer (Psalms 32:3–4).

Admitting his wrongs, however, brought David both physical and emotional refreshment:

> I acknowledged my sin to Thee,
> And my iniquity I did not hide;
> I said, "I will confess my transgression to the Lord";
> And Thou didst forgive the guilt of my sin.
> Thou art my hiding place;
> Thou dost preserve me from trouble;
> Thou dost surround me with songs of deliverance
> (Psalms 32:5, 7).

FORGIVENESS AND RESTITUTION

Forgiveness means releasing others from the debt of the wounds they have inflicted. It creates a renewed opportunity to base relationships on integrity and mutual respect. If others can accept forgiveness, then solid, lasting relationships can be built. If others continue to blame or control, they can still be forgiven, but their actions will hinder their relationships.

Joseph's life clearly illustrates forgiveness and restitution based on trust which was tested and found true. Joseph's brothers wanted to kill him, but instead, they sold him into slavery in Egypt. After being falsely accused of adultery, Joseph languished in a dungeon for many years. The Lord enabled Joseph to interpret the Pharaoh's dreams, and Joseph was then made prime minister of Egypt, second only to Pharaoh.

A severe famine devastated the land, just as Joseph had predicted, and his brothers came to Egypt looking for food, unaware that Joseph had been made prime minister. Before revealing his identity, Joseph tested his brothers to see if they would again forsake a brother as they had forsaken him. He secretly hid silver

. . .The sincerity of those who have been hurtful and controlling in the past can be "tested" to see if they are sincerely willing to have relationships based on trust and respect.

in their bags, caught them, and accused them of thievery. He insisted they leave Jacob's youngest son, Benjamin, as a hostage. After a long series of stern tests, Joseph was satisfied that he could trust his repentant brothers. He revealed his true identity as their brother, forgave them, and restored his relationship with them.

In the same way, the sincerity of those who have been hurtful and controlling in the past can be "tested" to see if they are sincerely willing to have relationships based on trust and respect. Patience and honesty can provide a foundation for trust to grow.

Forgiveness does not necessitate restitution. It provides a platform to develop a relationship if both parties are willing. Many people will insist on having relationships only on *their* terms. Their onslaught of manipulation (including accusations of *others'* selfish behavior) can cause people to revert to their subservient positions of being controlled again. Such relationships should be refused. However, the option to build a relationship established on respect and honesty can be offered.

Sometimes a person feels he or she cannot forgive someone else for a past offense. There are many ways a person can try to justify unforgiveness.

GOD'S PATIENCE

The Lord is very patient with us. He knows that we would be overwhelmed if we concurrently experienced all the pain we have repressed and all our sinfulness. So He metes out new self-perceptions of wounds and sins as people grow in their ability to handle them. As they progress in the healing process, they typically remark, "I had no idea I had so much anger in me," or, "I've just seen a whole lot of hurt that I've never seen before." One man told me, "I don't know how many layers of hurt, anger, and sin I've gone through, but I'm glad I didn't see all of this at the beginning! Every layer seems to be all I can take at that time. Sometimes I think God is harsh to let me go through all the pain, but then I realize that He is really patient to let me feel only as much as I can take."

As we forgive people completely for all the wounds we see they have caused, we also need to realize that the wounds may be deeper and uglier than we perceived at that point. In the early stages, we can forgive all we see; then we see more, and forgive them for that, too. As the layers continue to be peeled back and more wounds are exposed, we can continue to completely forgive all we see. "I used to be surprised when I saw that the wounds were deeper than I originally thought," a lady told me, "but now, I'm not surprised any more. I expect to find more; but at every layer, I feel more freedom and more able to give and receive love."

THE CHOICE TO FORGIVE

Forgiveness involves both grieving deeper losses as we become aware of them and being responsible to forgive those who inflicted the pain. As Philip Yancey's article says, forgiveness is "an unnatural act." Though experiencing Christ's forgiveness of us is the foundation and motivation for us to forgive others, the act of forgiveness is difficult and demands courage. And our forgiveness of others may or may not change them. They may soften and repent, or they may harden and continue to blame us. But the experience and expression of forgiveness *will* radically change us.

REFLECTION/DISCUSSION

1. In your own words describe the two errors (from this chapter) many Christians make in their attempts to forgive others.

2. Read Matthew 18:21–35. If the king represents God in this
    passage, and you and I are the first slave, then those who have
    wounded us represent the second slave. Draw the weight of
    our offenses toward God in relation to others' offenses toward
    us:

Which is bigger? How much bigger?

Do your offenses toward God seem bigger or smaller than
other offenses toward you? Why?

3. How would a more accurate understanding of your forgiveness
    by Christ help you forgive others?

4. In what way is our forgiveness of others a process? In what way is it a choice?

5. How does it help you to know that God is very patient with you as you learn to forgive?

[1] John R. W. Stott. *The Cross of Christ*, Downers Grove, IL: IVP, 1986, p. 297.

[2] Philip Yancey, "An Unnatural Act," *Christianity Today*, April 8, 1991, pp. 36–39.

15

◆

The Dynamic
of
Change

—Pat Springle

WHEN I BEGAN MY OWN HEALING PROCESS, I quickly saw that it would be very difficult to get healthy on my own. Now that I've been growing for a while, I can see that my perception was flawed. It's not *difficult* to get healthy by yourself; it's *impossible*.

We can learn a lot about our dysfunctions and behavioral patterns by reading books and going to seminars, but the give and take of close relationships provides the dynamic for genuine change. We may become riveted on one issue—the "key" to our health—but someone who has traveled the road before us can see that there are many essential elements to the healing process. These elements include safety, trust, risks, courage, honesty, grieving, responsibility, limits, time, and the work of God's Spirit in our lives. In this chapter, we will examine how a safe environment provides the encouragement we need to take risks and grow emotionally.

SAFETY

Threatening, unstable relationships often wound us while caring, stable relationships provide a safe environment for us to grow. However, many of us haven't the foggiest clue where to find nurturing relationships. We have been drawn to people who control s and dominate us, or who let us control and dominate them. We thought that people who said no to us were selfish, but we resented others who controlled us. One woman told me, "How do I find a good relationship? I've never been in one! I don't know what one looks like!"

A friend, a pastor, a counselor, or a small group can begin to show us what a true friend is like. We may have to look for a while, but sooner or later we will find people who:

- care about us but don't fix our problems

- listen but don't demand a certain response

- tell the truth without controlling us

- respect your identity without forcing you to be what they want you to be

- let us make our own decisions

- let us progress at our own rate

- let us feel, talk, and trust

- point us to the Lord's comfort and sovereignty

In that kind of relationship, trust can be established and growth encouraged.

RISKS

Some of us have sought help, risking our vulnerability only to get clobbered!

The safety that eluded many of us as children can still be experienced in the family of God. "Wait a minute!" some of us might say. "Some of my deepest wounds and disappointments are from Christians who didn't understand me. I've given up on Christians. I still love God, but Christians. . . . I don't think I can trust anybody. It's easier to just be alone." Some of us have sought help, risking our vulnerability only to get clobbered! Perhaps someone told us how to feel, that we needed to forget the past and move on, or another person broke confidentiality and shared our problem as a "prayer request."

Whether we are taking the risk to get into a healing relationship for the first time or rebounding from "being burned" by a bad experience, several principles apply:

Be wise in selecting—Many of us are so hungry for love that we jump at the first chance we see. We need to learn the true nature of a person or group with whom we are considering getting involved. Most non-church based groups talk in general terms about spirituality, but they may promote New Age philosophies or Eastern mysticism. The content should be clearly Christian, and the context should also be focused on Christian characteristics. It is wise to observe someone or attend a group for a while to establish its trustworthiness.

Have the courage to be vulnerable—When we feel relatively confident that the person or group is worthy of our trust, we can begin to tell our stories. Some of us can tell our stories all at once. Others can only tell a little at a time. The choice to portion out the story may be due to fear, or we may simply not be able to remember events and feelings because we have repressed them. We have to get healthier to remember the pain.

Tenacity to keep going—No matter how gifted a friend or counselor may be, no matter how good a group is, fallen people meeting with fallen people inevitably cause disappointment. Most of these situations can be worked through. We forgive, grieve, and learn. Sometimes we realize that we may need to try another group. However, we must be careful not to "group hop," looking for people to tell us what we want to hear. An objective, mature person can help us determine if our struggles are a part of the healing process or a hindrance to it.

All of us get tired of the healing process from time to time, whether our friend or group is wonderful or not. "I'm burned out on healing," one man told me. "I'm so tired of seeing buried wounds and grieving them, struggling to make new decisions, and all that.

I need a break!" Several years ago, I broke my wrist. For a few days, the novelty of a cast occupied my attention, but making allowances for it soon proved to be a grind. I was tired of it! But I had very little choice; I had to continue the process if I wanted my wrist to get well. Similarly, we may get tired of the focused attention, time commitment and cumbersome emotional toll of healing our emotional wounds. Though we may need to take a short break occasionally, we need tenacity to keep going. The benefits of trusting and growing can be erased if we don't keep taking those risks when they aren't exciting anymore.

SUPPORT GROUPS

Many people have commented that "the lights came on" in their lives as they listened to others describe their family struggles, new perceptions, and hard choices.

One-to-one friendships or counseling are tremendously valuable, but the added environment of a small group can spur increased growth. Many people have commented that "the lights came on" in their lives as they listened to others describe their family struggles, new perceptions, and hard choices. One woman told her group: "All this time I thought I was the only one who had these problems. I felt so alone, but since I've been coming here, I've realized that other people feel just like me! And many of them have made real progress. Now I have hope that I can grow, too!"

Support groups are expressly designed to accomplish the goals of the healing process by establishing trust relationships as the foundation for developing healthy, mature adult-adult relationships. In *Theory and Practice of Group Counseling*, Gerald Corey writes:

> One of the main reasons for the popularity of the group as a primary therapeutic tool in many agencies and institutions is that the group approach is frequently more

effective than individual approaches. This is due to the fact that group members can practice new skills both in the group and in their everyday interactions outside of it.[1]

Though Christ modeled small group ministry with the disciples, the church has only recently assumed its rightful leadership role in providing support groups to "bind up the broken-hearted." A recent issue of *Discipleship Journal* was devoted to the examination of small groups. An article on "A Brief History of Small Groups" by Jim and Carol Plueddemann concludes:

> Whereas most of the small group movement of the sixties and early seventies took place outside of church structures and even in reaction to the institutional church, today that picture has changed dramatically. Small group ministries are proliferating within the church and as outreaches from the church. Many pastors and congregations are intentionally developing a variety of small group ministries as the core of their church life.[2]

Church-based growth groups and support groups are great environments for Christ-centered emotional healing. They aren't perfect because Christians aren't perfect, but they have proven successful in millions of lives.

GROWING UP

Rob had been depressed for several years, but finally he sought help. Antidepressants had given him a clearer mind so he could think and choose more wisely. Through his counselor, he realized that his depression had been caused by repressed anger. His parents had pressured him to perform, and he had done exceptionally well in academics and athletics. But no matter how well he did, he never received the affirmation he needed and wanted. The pressure finally got to him when an employer treated him the same way. Tension grew; his stomach became chronically upset, and finally, he became lethargic and ceased to function normally. "I'd wake up in the morning dreading to get up. My body felt like it weighed 800 pounds. I'd drag myself through the day the best I could, but it was a real pain. I don't know how long I would have kept on that way if my brother hadn't told me to get some help."

Rob's counselor provided a safe environment for him to feel again—only the feelings weren't too pleasant. They hurt. After the initial wave of anger and sadness, Rob began to feel hopeful. He began to have some fun and laugh. He grew in his confidence to make decisions. "I feel like a kid!" he told his counselor. "I haven't felt this way in a long time—if ever!"

> *"I sure wish I had learned all those things when I was a kid, but I guess I'll have to learn them now."*

He still had a long way to go to grieve the wounds of the past and become a responsible adult, but Rob had grasped the essence of change: it's like growing up. We can still learn the life-skills we were supposed to acquire in the context of our families. Rob reflected, "I sure wish I had learned all those things when I was a kid, but I guess I'll have to learn them now."

The Apostle Paul believed the goal of church leadership is to provide instruction and encouragement (Ephesians 4:13). The fruit of this environment is the growth of individuals from spiritual and emotional childhood to adulthood. "As a result, we are no longer to be children, tossed here and there by waves, and carried about by every wind of doctrine, by the trickery of men, by craftiness in deceitful scheming (Ephesians 4:14).

This growth is to be accomplished in the supportive and strengthening environment of loving, honest relationships:

> But speaking the truth in love, we are to grow up in all aspects into Him, who is the head, even Christ,
> From whom the whole body, being fitted and held together by that which every joint supplies, according to the proper working of each individual part, causes the growth of the body for the building up of itself in love (Ephesians 4:15–16).

People who receive counseling sometimes say they feel like children as they get in touch with their repressed hurt and anger. Some actually revert to child-like physical mannerisms, behaviors, and speech patterns as they describe the deep wounds of their past. Many authorities state that significant traumas, such as abuse or neglect, effectively "block" a person's emotional development while the body continues to mature. Certain social progress can still be attained, but the ability to cope emotionally with difficult people or stressful situations may be hindered. The person may, in fact, deal with these problems in much the same way as he would have at the time his development was blocked. Even successful lawyers, housewives, plumbers, and sales clerks may act like toddlers throwing tantrums when things don't go their way. Or they may withdraw and hide in fear like young children instead of facing the adversity.

A very popular concept of emotional growth today is the "inner child movement." Many popular secular authors and speakers, most notably John Bradshaw, are using this approach to illustrate a person whose emotional development has been blocked at some point. This is a wonderful and powerful metaphor, but I have significant reservations about it.

The positive elements of the "inner child" metaphor include:

- It enables a person to detach and to be more objective about his wounds.

- People are encouraged to "adopt" their "inner child." This encourages a sense of nurturing and protecting which was painfully absent in the person's childhood.

- The metaphor is validated by many authors and lecturers in the secular recovery movement and increasingly in certain elements of the Christian recovery movement as well.

- Many people give powerful testimonies of how their "inner child work" has brought catharsis and progress into their lives. But depending on the communicator, serious flaws or at least considerable red flag issues are found in this concept.

The "inner child" metaphor is more closely associated with non-biblical (and even anti-biblical) principles. Its origin is found in Eric Berne's Transactional Analysis psychological paradigm.[3]

Bradshaw relates "inner child work" to Zen Buddhism. Furthermore many of the exercises of mind release and styles of meditation are more common to the New Age movement than to a biblical approach.[4]

Some major proponents of the concept communicate that the "inner child" is perfect,[5] and as we allow the inner child to heal and grow, we will become perfect, too. Perfection is a common theme in New Age philosophy, but it is clearly unbiblical.

Also, some leaders of the movement encourage followers to accept their homosexual inner child or lesbian inner child or some other sinful behavior, without mentioning the need for repentance. Acceptance, of course, sounds positive and loving, but blind acceptance of sinful behavior does not lead to a healthy, biblically-based life.

"Adopting your inner child," that is, thinking of yourself as outside yourself, can promote dissociation rather than integration. *It is not someone else who was wounded,* one man reflected. *It was me!* Proponents argue that integration of the person is the ultimate goal and the increased objectivity makes the risk of dissociation worthwhile, but the risk is substantial.

These paragraphs are not meant to be a scathing polemic on the "inner child movement." But the considerable number of negatives concerning its origin and basic philosophy should give us cause to avoid using this concept.

The concept of adoption is a thoroughly biblical and powerful truth which contains the positive elements of the "inner child" philosophy without the negatives. The Apostle Paul wrote eloquently to the believers in Rome of the contrast between our slavery to sin's consequences of hurt and fear and the new relationship of love and protection we have as children of God:

> For you have not received a spirit of slavery leading to fear
> again, but you have received a spirit of adoption as sons by
> which we cry out, "Abba! Father!" (Romans 8:15).

In his masterpiece of Christian experience, *Knowing God,* J.I. Packer writes:

> The New Testament gives us two yardsticks for measuring
> God's love. The first is the cross (see Romans 5:8; 1 John
> 4:8–10); the second is the gift of sonship. "Behold, what

manner of love the Father has bestowed upon us, that we should be called the sons of God!" (1 John 3:1, RSV). Of all the gifts of grace, adoption is the highest.[6]

*A*doption, by its very nature, is an act of free kindness to the person adopted.

Packer goes on to say:

Adoption, by its very nature, is an act of free kindness to the person adopted. If you become a father by adopting a child, you do so because you choose to, not because you are bound to. Similarly, God adopts because He chooses to. He had no duty to do so. He need not have done anything about our sins save punish us as we deserved. But He loved us; so He redeemed us, forgave us, took us as His sons, and give Himself to us as our Father.[7]

Another scholar and theologian, John R.W. Stott, writes of the emotional catharsis of experiencing our adoption by God:

One of the most satisfying aspects of the gospel is the way in which it combines the objective and the subjective, the historical and the experimental, the work of God's son and the work of God's Spirit. We may know that God loves us, Paul says, both because he has proved his love in history through the death of his Son, and because he continuously pours it into our hearts through the indwelling of his spirit. And although we shall concentrate, as Paul does, on the objective demonstration of God's love at the cross, we shall not forget that the Holy Spirit confirms that historical witness by his own inward and personal witness, as he floods our hearts with the knowledge that we are loved.[8]

Our adoption by a loving Father also puts us into relationships with His family, and though many of His children are painfully dysfunctional, other brothers and sisters in Christ can provide the warmth, affection, and honesty we all need. We are not alone.

REFLECTION/DISCUSSION

1. In your opinion, what are some characteristics of a "safe environment"?

2. Have you ever experienced one? If so, when? How did you respond to it?

3. Look up several of the "one another" passages in your Bible to see them in context. Paraphrase them here:

   • love one another (1 John 4:11)

   • accept one anther (Romans 15:7)

   • forgive one another (Colossians 3:13, Ephesians 4:32)

   • encourage one another (1 Thessalonians 5:11, Hebrews 10:24)

   • confess to one another (James 5:16)

   • serve one another (1 Peter 4:10)

   • admonish one another (1 Thessalonians 5:14)

   • pray for one another (James 5:16)

4. What might happen if a group of people genuinely experienced these kinds of relationships?

5. Trust always involves risks. What risks are you willing to take to have more meaningful relationship? How do you feel about those risks?

6. Paraphrase Romans 8:15.

7. How do you feel about your adoption by God?

8. How can your adoption help you feel more secure so that you can have more courage to take risks?

[1] Gerald Corey. *Theory and Practice of Group Counseling*, Monterey, CA: Brooks/Cole Publishing Co., 1981, p. 4.

[2] Jim and Carol Pluedemann. "A Brief History of Small Groups" *Discipleship Journal*, September/October, 1990, (Vol. 10, Number 5, p. 21).

[3] Eric Berne. *Games People Play*, New York: Ballentine, 1978.

[4] John Bradshaw. *The Homecoming*, New York: Bantam, 1990.

[5] Charles Whitfield, M.D. *Healing the Child Within,* Deerfield Beach, Fl: Healthcare, Inc.

[6] J.I. Packer. *Knowing God*, Downers Grove, IL: IV Press, 1973, p. 194.

[7] Ibid., p. 195.

[8] John R.W. Stott. *The Cross of Christ*, Downers Grove, IL: IV Press, 1986, p. 213.

Section Three

16

◆

Explosions
and
Reactions

—Pat Springle

In the spring of 1980, geologists noticed distinct rumblings deep within Mount St. Helens. The mountain had erupted many times during the past several hundred years, though not since 1857. But pressure was building. From all appearances, the scene seemed serene and peaceful, but inside, an explosion was preparing to be unleashed. Then on the morning of May 18, 1981, the top third of the mountain suddenly blew off in a cataclysmic explosion of rock, lava, and ash. Hundreds of square miles of timber were leveled in seconds. The sky was darkened for thousands of miles by the choking, smothering volcanic dust. The pressure required for such an explosion was calculated to be as much as 100 times that of the atomic bomb dropped on Hiroshima. This pressure had built for years; then finally it blew.

Many people who go through the process of emotional healing describe their experience in similar terms: years of repressed emotions that accumulate pressure until those compacted feelings erupt uncontrollably. Joseph related:

For years I tried to cover up the pain. I tried to excel—and I did for a while. I drank during one period, but that only created more problems. Finally, I became depressed—*really* depressed. For several years I tried to fight it. I made excuses for my lethargy and bad attitude. My relationship with my wife and kids got worse. Then I got help. The counselor helped me go back to some root problems, and when I began to talk about my family, I felt things I hadn't felt in years! I was *furious* about the way I'd been treated—all the control and abuse. Many times I wanted to put the lid on again because it hurt so bad, but I kept going.

. . . *Before we begin the healing process, these eruptions are anything but cathartic. They are devastating, and leave us in the quagmire of shame, self-hatred, loneliness, and confusion.*

Many of us "erupt" before we begin the healing process. Outbursts of anger or deep feelings of hurt seem to spurt out even when we try to rigidly control ourselves. And before we begin the healing process, these eruptions are anything but cathartic. They are devastating, and leave us in the quagmire of shame, self-hatred, loneliness, and confusion. Our outbursts can be uncontrolled and frightening, both before and after we begin the healing process. The difference is that without help, they can cause even more repression and pressure. But as a first step toward recovery, they lead us toward health and growth.

The phases of the healing process described in this section are not comprehensive. They will not detail every issue and nuance of emotional healing for depression, chemical abuse, codependency, eating disorders, sexual abuse, and other problems. These difficulties are specifically addressed in other books.

The chapters that follow describe the general flow of a person's progress toward trust, responsibility, boundaries, identity, and intimacy. Specific responses may vary from person to person.

An irresponsible, chemically dependent person may need to change in quite a different fashion than an overly responsible codependent. A clinically depressed person's reaction will not be the same as someone who is compulsively driven.

Nor is there a set time frame for these phases. Many factors determine a person's rate of progress: the presence or absence of a nurturing environment, courage, the depth of the wound, complicating circumstances such as debt or divorce, the priority of time and attention to the healing process, God's timing, and so forth. Some people take years to become aware of their pain and desperate enough to do something about it. Others act quickly when they finally see the opportunity to trust someone and talk about their wounds.

Grieving over wounds and taking responsibility may seem easy to some people. Like fixing an engine or solving a math problem, there are principles to help us accomplish what we're trying to do. But many of us don't even know where the engine is or what page the problem is on. And when we do finally get started, we generally have to unlearn skills which prevent problem solving before we acquire new, needed skills.

A young man recently called to say that he had read one of the books published by our organization. He told us he was expecting to get over his depression and compulsive drivenness in a week or so. I replied, "I'm glad you benefited from the book and that you are learning a lot. That's great! But healing might take a little longer than you expect."

WHY BEGIN?

I have asked many people why they waited so long to start the process of emotional healing. Many of them listed reasons which kept them mired in denial, such as emotional inertia, fear of betraying the family, fear of feeling the deep hurt they suspect is buried within them, fear of the unknown, fear of being weird or out of control, and a host of other reasons. Beth told me, "The pain involved in getting healthy seemed greater than the pain of staying and letting myself be manipulated, so I stayed."

What she says is also true for many others. The setup of many family systems tends to reward those who remain puppets in their roles. The system punishes independence, change, and growth.

There are lots of reasons for not getting started in the emotional healing process, but people consistently mention one reason to take the first step—desperation. "I just can't live like this anymore," a lady in our group stated emphatically. *"I have got to get some help!"*

EXPRESSIONS OF DESPERATION

- "I've been depressed so long. . . . Surely *somebody* can help me."
- "My life is a wreck! I've given and given to other people. . . . Now I'm empty, in debt, and alone."
- "I can't stand the hurt any longer. Either I'm going to get help or. . . ."
- "My bitterness toward my first wife has ruined my relationship with my second wife, as well as every other relationship in my life. Something has got to change!"
- "My temper is out of control. Sometimes I hit things and want to hurt people. I'm afraid of what I might do to my children."
- "After the divorce, I felt so ashamed. Since then I've not made any progress. If I don't get started soon, I'll just die."
- "I never thought my parents' divorce affected me that much, but now I'm thinking about getting married and I'm afraid it won't last. I want to get close, but I also want to run. Who can help me?"
- "When I lost my job, my self-concept went through the floor. I feel like a total flop, going nowhere fast."
- "Now that my mother is sick, the strain on me is taking a heavy toll. She pouts like a child if I don't do whatever she wants. I've given out until I'm a dry well."
- "I thought I could get over his death, but time hasn't helped that much. There must be more to it than this!"
- "When I look at my children and see that I treat them exactly the way my father treated me, I can't stand it! I hate the way he treated me, and I hate myself for treating them that way. What can I do?"

The initial realizations of our hurts often put us in an awkward state of limbo between *I have a problem* and *I need to get help.* The recognition that something is wrong has yet to blossom into the desperation that "I can't live like this any longer."

We often rationalize hurt: "She didn't mean it." "He couldn't help it." "It really wasn't that bad." The ebb and flow of realization and rationalization can last for weeks, months, or even years. But finally, the level of desperation rises above the level of fear and we take the first step to get help.

FIRST STEPS

Some of us take a first step by buying and reading (secretly) some book on emotional healing. We exhibit a level of trust in the author—not much, perhaps, but at least enough to see what he has to say. Yet reading a book frequently raises more questions than it answers. A wealth of information with little or no implementation leads to confusion.

But if we don't get stuck at this point, what we read may inspire us to talk to someone whom we feel is safe: a pastor, a Sunday school teacher, or a friend. This presents a whole new group of ways to get stuck. Our comments or questions may be phrased strangely. The person may not understand the overwhelming sense of desperation we feel. Or perhaps the person offers bad advice: "You shouldn't feel that way;" "Oh, that's not so bad. Let me tell you about my wife's problems;" or "Man, that's too bad. I wouldn't tell anybody about that!" If we receive superficial, insensitive answers at this point, we may get stuck before we even get started. Any fear of being rejected may be intensified through such an interaction, and it may be months until we get desperate enough to try again.

Finding a safe person is the critical step at this point. We may have to try talking to several people, but eventually we will find someone we can talk to without fear of rejection. At first it is very difficult to risk trusting even the most trustworthy people. We are cautious as we begin to disclose our situation or reveal the "family secret." But what comes out in bits and pieces at first may soon become a Pandora's box of repressed feelings.

The confusion, guilt, and conflicting emotions at this point can be overwhelming. A nurturing person or group provides a safe environment to take the risk of being vulnerable and talking more openly.

"I realized that I had to talk about it if I was going to make progress," Mary said. "I kept excusing my husband for his drinking, blaming myself for his irresponsibility, and feeling guilty for talking about it at all!"

Dean had come to a group several times without participating in the conversation. He listened intently and we let him assimilate without demanding a response. But eventually he asked if he could ask a question. "Of course," the leader responded.

"Are you saying that my background has something to do with the hurt I feel?"

"Yes," the leader responded, "our family background often plays a major role in our emotional well-being and relationships."

Dean looked uncomfortable but determined. He said, "My mother was an alcoholic. Can that have any impact on my life?"

Though it was the most elementary of observations, no one laughed. Several people explained how an alcoholic parent had affected them. Since Dean felt safe, he had risked asking a personal question. His risk was rewarded by those whose answers affirmed his perceptions and feelings. Over the next several months, Dean became an active participant in the group and made progress.

Identifying one or two elements of dysfunction in our lives can be difficult, but realizing the extensive patterns of repressed hurts, defense mechanisms, and painful consequences can be terrifying! Many people stop before they reach that point. Their progress is blocked because, while they are willing to admit "a little problem," they are unable or unwilling to continue into the deep water of facing the reality of severe hurts and imbedded anger. They resist the "eruption" of emotions that takes place when someone finally come to grips with the reality of his pain.

EMOTIONAL EXPLOSIONS

Like Mount St. Helens, we seem to explode with the release of accumulated anger, hurt, bitterness, and fear. People who come face-to-face with pain after repressing it for years speak of the experience as "overwhelming," "out of control," or "terrifying."

"I had no idea all of that was in there," a pastor's wife told me. "For years I lived without acknowledging the pain of feeling abandoned by my father. I tried to be the best wife I could be, but I never seemed to be able to empathize with depressed people. I told them to 'get a grip on yourself,' because that's what I tried to do. But when I began to feel the hurt, I almost couldn't take it. I thought I'd die."

As he talked about being manipulated by his mother, I realized—suddenly—that my mother had never trusted me to make my own decisions. She had controlled me. Out of nowhere I became livid!

Others describe the release of intense anger. "I had been in a Bible study for two years," a man related, "but I didn't start dealing with my past until a new guy joined our group. He talked about the repressed hurt and anger he had been dealing with. Several of us asked questions, and something in me snapped. As he talked about being manipulated by his mother, I realized—suddenly—that my mother had never trusted me to make my own decisions. She had controlled me. Out of nowhere I became livid! I was so angry at my mother I could spit nails, but I was also shocked and afraid that so much venom was coming out of me. I had to leave the group and go for a drive to try to cool off, but I only became more enraged."

When confronted with their own anger, most conscientious Christians are quickly stopped by the thought that they should avoid getting angry because anger is a sin. At this crucial juncture they often choose to repress their feelings rather than confronting the problem, dealing with the anger, and moving ahead from there.

"I remember quite vividly," Rich related, "when I had to choose between continuing to repress my anger or being honest about it. I guess the Lord put it in my mind at that moment that I would never get healthy if I continued to push it down and act like it wasn't there. That was an important point for me."

We are taught to suppress "negative" feelings. We are

taught that only positive emotions are okay. Many of us learn in church that we can't be angry and be "good Christians." With all we have been told, we have difficulty realizing that feelings aren't wrong. Feelings are neutral. They reflect our perception of the environment around us. Our behaviors may be either right or wrong, but our feelings are neither. Instead of repressing emotions, we can "own them," accept them, and learn from them. Accepting our feelings is another crucial step in the journey toward emotional health.

REACTIONS

Just as our emotions go from one extreme to another (from repression to explosion), so will our outer reactions. Whatever beliefs we have clung to may change. However we acted before, we behave differently now. We changed . . .

- . . . from self-pity to blaming others
- . . . from acquiescence to rebellion
- . . . from confusion to knowing what needs to be done
- . . . from grandioseness to depression
- . . . from numbness to rage
- . . . from, "I'm not going to talk about this" to, "I'm going to tell him off"
- . . . from, "My friends understand me" to, "My friends don't understand me"
- . . . from lethargy to activity
- . . . from trusting too much to trusting no one
- . . . from feeling indispensable to feeling worthless
- . . . from, "Nobody cares about me" to, "These are the best friends in the world"
- . . . from, "My family is wonderful" to, "My family is awful"
- . . . from, "My problems are minor" to, "My problems are monumental"

As we begin to shift from repressing our feelings to expressing them, our outer reactions ricochet back and forth, propelled in one direction by intense hurt and anger and another direction by guilt. Our black-or-white mind-sets cause us to overreact for months (or longer) until identity and perceptions become more stabilized.

One of the richest sources of honest expression of emotions is the Book of Psalms. Look at the anguish and hopelessness expressed by the psalmist:

> I will say to God my rock, "Why hast Thou forgotten me? Why do I go mourning because of the oppression of the enemy?"
> As a shattering of my bones, my adversaries revile me, while they say to me all day long, "Where is your God?" (Psalms 42:9–10)

And when David felt deeply grieved over his sins and inadequacies, he lamented:

> Be gracious to me, O Lord, for I am pining away; heal me, O Lord, for my bones are dismayed.
> And my soul is greatly dismayed; but Thou, O Lord—how long?
> I am weary with my sighing; every night I make my bed swim, I dissolve my couch with my tears.
> My eye has wasted away with grief; it has become old because of all my adversaries (Psalms 6:2–3, 6–7).

Yet David was assured that God heard him, understood him, forgave him, and would ultimately protect him:

> The Lord has heard my supplication, the Lord receives my prayer.
> All my enemies shall be ashamed and greatly dismayed; they shall turn back, they shall suddenly be ashamed (Psalms 6:9–10).

REAL PROGRESS

When a person first begins to experience emotional explosions and strong reactions, it's not unusual to think that this is exactly the opposite of growth and healing. We seem to be getting worse! "I want to feel *good*, not like *this*!" a woman told her group leader. "Is *this* progress?"

"Sometimes you have to get worse before you get better," the leader responded.

"How much worse?" she replied. "I don't think I ever would have started if I'd known it was going to be this hard."

"*We* enter the process out of desperation.
We continue it out of hope."

The leader answered, "Do you remember how you felt and what you said when you started coming here? You said, 'I'll do *anything* to get better and to heal the wounds I feel.' Now you're going through one of those times that everybody in the process experiences: a time when your old props have been taken away and you haven't yet replaced them with new ones. Times like these are hard; they're awkward." Then he said, "We enter the process out of desperation. We continue it out of hope. You are making real progress, even if you can't see it. Don't stop now."

REFLECTION/DISCUSSION
1. Explain some reasons you felt (feel) desperate enough to begin your healing process.

2. If you have begun the healing process:

   • What explosions have you experienced as you uncovered buried emotions?

   • How did you feel about yourself when you experienced these explosions?

- How did you react toward the people involved? Toward others?

3. Do you believe emotional "pendulum swings" are normal in the healing process? Why or why not?

4. Many people get confused and impatient as they experience these explosions and reactions. How can you tell if you are making real progress?

5. How would you respond if it felt that you were going backward?

6. Paraphrase Psalm 73:21–26.

   How does this passage relate to "explosions and reactions"?

17

◆

Critical
Decisions

—Robert S. McGee

RECENTLY I WATCHED A PBS PROGRAM that showed people rock climbing at Yosemite National Park. The park contains El Capitán, one of the most challenging, straight-up rock faces in the country. Each step up the precipice required careful observation, analysis, risk, and effort. At each precarious point, the climber looks for the best place to drive a piton or grab a handhold. Then he takes the risk of shifting his weight to the new position. If his observation, choice, and technique are good enough, he is secure. If not, or if his grip slips, he can have a frightening fall until the safety rope stops him.

A few falls make climbers very careful! Progress up the cliff is very slow and methodical. Every step is crucial. Each one entails risks and rewards.

In the same way, progress toward emotional healing requires careful observation, analysis, risk, and effort. Each decision is a potential step forward. Though no single step seems like much on its own, and discouragement can easily sap our motivation, steady progress can be made.

As the first phase of emotional explosions and reactions start to subside, a second phase of growth begins. This phase is marked by big decisions, significant changes, and potentially tremendous progress. A hundred choices, large and small, confront us every day. Every situation and interaction is an opportunity for growth, for consolidating gains, for making new strides—or for falling back a step or two. This second phase of growth is often characterized by the phrase, "Three steps forward and two steps back." Like climbing a mountain, progress is difficult . . . but rewarding.

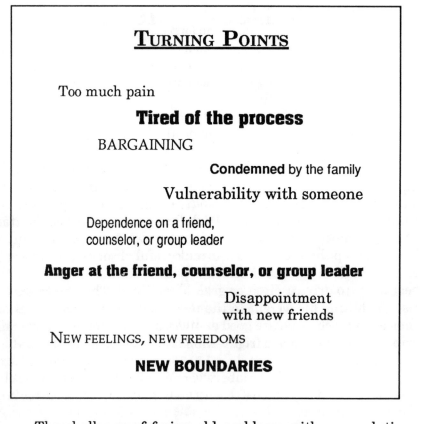

TURNING POINTS

Too much pain

Tired of the process

BARGAINING

Condemned by the family

Vulnerability with someone

Dependence on a friend,
counselor, or group leader

Anger at the friend, counselor, or group leader

Disappointment
with new friends

NEW FEELINGS, NEW FREEDOMS

NEW BOUNDARIES

The challenge of facing old problems with new solutions leads us to many turning points which determine whether we continue to proceed, slow down, or get stuck. Some of these factors are listed on the chart and detailed below.

Too much pain—As people get farther along into the healing process, many lament, "I never thought it would be this hard." As our tried and true defense mechanisms slowly come down, underneath them we find hurt, hatred, loneliness, and a host of other goblins in all their gory glory. We go through the cycle of perceiving pain, grieving, and experiencing comfort. With each cycle we go a little deeper and think, *Surely this is the worst it can get!*

Tired of the process—We get discouraged and disappointed. We feel like we've done all we can do, but the hurt is still there. We think, *I thought I'd be well by now. I'm really tired of this.* We echo David's expression of disappointment:

> How long, O Lord? Wilt Thou forget me forever? How long wilt Thou hide Thy face from me?
> How long shall I take counsel in my soul, having sorrow in my heart all the day? How long will my enemy be exalted over me?
> Consider and answer me, O Lord, my God; enlighten my eyes, lest I sleep the sleep of death (Psalms 13:1–3).

Bargaining—Sooner or later, we realize that we can't bargain with those who have hurt us. The logical response to the reality of our wounds is typically, *Then how can I get them to love me?* But attempts to trade something else for love only intensifies their manipulation of us. When we realize we are still bargaining, we may either adopt a sense of abandonment or become furious at those who have wounded us.

Condemned by the family—Tired of bargaining, many of us determine to confront the offenders, expecting those people to admit their offenses and repent. But our expectations are usually naive. It is very likely that the offenders will "turn up the heat" of manipulation and condemnation in an attempt to maintain control.

Vulnerability with someone—Most of us have several check points in our ability to experience feelings and willingness to share them with others. We may not be able to communicate the depth of our wounds. We may not trust anyone enough to express all we feel. It's perfectly fine to decide when and how to take the next step, because each one is a new level of risk and vulnerability. One man mentioned to his group, "I've told you folks more than I ever imagined I'd tell anybody, but there are several things I can't talk about yet. I'm not ready right now."

Dependence on a friend, counselor, or group leader—"Nobody has ever understood me before. I don't know what I'd do without you." These thoughts and feelings are often expressed by people whose hurts are finally being comforted by another person. In the earliest stages, as trust is first developed, some dependency may be necessary and unavoidable, but prolonged dependency should be avoided. Be aware that some friends and group leaders have codependent needs to feel needed, but too much dependence on them short-circuits further growth for the person being "helped."

Anger at the friend, counselor, or group leader—Sometimes hurting people *want* to be dependent on the person helping them. They become angry when the helping person doesn't meet every need or expectation. Honesty about dysfunctions can hurt, even when communicated in love. As a result, many transfer the pain they have experienced from others onto those who seek to help them.

Disappointment with new friends—As we begin to develop new relationships, we may expect our new friends to be perfect—or close to it. We are deeply disappointed to discover they have flaws. "I thought the people in this group would be a lot different, but they're just like me," a lady stated sardonically.

New feelings, new freedoms—As long-repressed emotions come to the surface, we learn to grieve them. Only then do we discover that along with the anger and hurt, we may have also awakened other dormant feelings—happiness, freedom, sexual desire, and so forth. At times we may feel like a kid with a new toy! We feel exhilarated, though often it takes a while to appreciate our new freedom and desires because we're still dealing with past guilt and rigidity.

New boundaries—Every day we have many opportunities to make decisions regarding feelings, desires, behaviors, and relationships. We learn to say no to the compulsive things we used to do. We learn to say yes to healthy things we have avoided. We tell people the truth instead of skirting it. We decide what our priorities and schedule should be instead of doing what others demand. We also take responsibility for our behavior, and we let others experience the consequences of theirs.

All of the previous turning points provide choices. Some are clear. Some may remain muddy for a while. Some require additional grieving of losses. Others need firm decisions and definitive action.

NEW PERCEPTIONS

At some point in the healing process, we reach the great revelation that we actually *do* have choices. Frank commented, "All my life I operated on the assumption that I had to do things, or else."

I asked, "Or else what?"

"Or else . . . I don't know exactly. Or else I would be condemned? Or else I would feel guilty? But I never thought I had choices. There was only one: do it or else!"

As perception improves and stability grows, the extremes of black-or-white thinking abate and the driving factors of fear and guilt diminish. We become able to see "gray" in people and situations, and with the moderated perception comes a broader array of options.

"I used to think that I had to do whatever my wife wanted," James reflected. "I was driven to please her. I felt so angry and tense, but I didn't know any other way to live. As I've gotten healthier I see that I have lots more options. He showed me a list of choices he could make:

- I can disagree with her and talk to her about it.

- I can let her be angry with me instead of doing whatever I can to please her.

- I can tell her what my ideas are.

- I can feel my hurt and anger, and then respond appropriately instead of suppressing my feelings and blowing up or becoming depressed.

- I can get us to go to a marriage counselor or a seminar on communication.

- I can be myself without being ashamed, afraid, or guilty!

We usually enter the healing process with the perception of having very few options. Many of us have abdicated our choices in order to escape responsibility. A breakthrough occurs when we realize that we actually have many alternatives to choose from. Our choices, though, also entail responsibility. As our sense of security grows, so will our ability to accept responsibility.

HANDLES

"How do I know what my choices are?" an exasperated person asked his group members. "You talk about making my own choices. What are they?"

In *Codependency: A Christian Perspective* (Rapha/Word), handles are assigned to the decision-making process.[1] These handles are applicable to all kinds of issues, not just codependency. The three main handles we use are: Identify, Detach, and Decide.

Identify—You can't hit a nail with a hammer if you can't see the nail. We must learn to identify dysfunctional behaviors, thoughts, and feelings if we expect to change them. As we learn to recognize our own cravings, fear, shame, hatred, depression, control, hurt, withdrawal, defense mechanisms, and so forth, then we can do something about them and experience repentance and freedom. The inability to identify these things leaves us in their grip without much hope of change.

Detach—When we identify an issue in our lives, we should step back physically and emotionally, and seek to be as objective as possible. We need emotional space to be able to think clearly and sort out our feelings. Sometimes we need to get away from the offending person for a while so we can become more objective. Some questions which can help us at such times include:

- Why did he say (do) that to me?

- What did he mean?

- How do I feel about it?

- How would a healthy person feel?

- Is he controlling me? Condemning me? Neglecting me?

- Why do I feel guilty? Driven? Afraid? Lonely?

- Am I rescuing someone?

- Am I acting as a savior? A Judas?

Certain statements may also be useful in helping us become more objective:

- I'm not responsible for making him happy.

- I'm not responsible for fixing the problem.

- He needs to be responsible for himself.

- I can respond calmly.

- I can say no.

- I can say yes.

- I can make my own decisions.

- I feel angry . . . lonely . . . guilty . . . driven . . . afraid.

- I am loved, forgiven, and accepted by God through Jesus Christ.

Decide—Identifying the problem and becoming objectively detached are of little value if we don't act on what we discover. Plans can seem simple and logical when we are alone, but terrifying when we actually begin to follow through on them. We need courage, and the support of others can be instrumental. To go back to our analogy of rock climbing, we can say that *deciding* is like the climber shifting his weight. It involves the greatest risk as well as the greatest rewards. A few statements that communicate our decisiveness to others include:

- This is what I will do. This is what I won't do.

- I will not tolerate this kind of behavior any more.

- I'm not responsible for his happiness.

- I refuse to be manipulated.

- I'm sorry, I wish I could help you, but I can't.

- Why did you say that to me? Do you know how I feel when you say things like that?

- I don't want to talk about this.
- I want to talk about this.

Though the apostle Paul did not have emotional healing specifically in mind when he wrote to the believers in Ephesus, his broader concept of repentance certainly reflects the principles of identifying, detaching, and deciding. He wrote:

> You were taught, with regard to your former way of life, to put off your old self, which is being corrupted by its deceitful desires;
> To be made new in the attitude of your minds;
> And to put on the new self, created to be like God in true righteousness and holiness (Ephesians 4:22–24, NIV).

The renewal of our minds based on the Word of God detaches us from established habits and enables us to form new perspectives on ourselves, others, and situations.

A person is unable to "put off" something unless he can *identify* it. The renewal of our minds based on the Word of God detaches us from established habits and enables us to form new perspectives on ourselves, others, and situations. Then, "putting on the new self" involves *deciding* to establish new, healthy, positive ways of relating to God and other people.

Identify, Detach, and Decide: These handles can be instrumental in helping a person make genuine progress day after day.

ACCEPTING THE PROCESS

A man in a support group shook his head and said, "I'm 43 years old. I sure wish I'd known all this when I was younger! I'd have saved myself a lot of pain—and I'd have saved many other people a lot of pain, too."

Another person piped in, "Well, I wish I had learned these things when I was 43! I'm almost 60." Several people laughed, but it wasn't really a joke.

The "I wish's" and the "might-have-been's" can rob us of strength for the climb. A significant step in this phase of development is the ability to accept ourselves where we are and not get stuck in self-pity or self-condemnation for not being farther along.

The Lord is supremely patient. He doesn't demand that we "get over it all" in an instant. He understands that comfort is experienced over a period of time, and changes in the fundamental patterns of our responsibilities and relationships occur slowly. And since He accepts us in the middle of the process, maybe we can, too.

A friend once said, "God is pleased with the process." Our walk of faith with Him is not one that focuses only on the end result and expects perfection. God is pleased when we courageously take strides, when we trust Him for wisdom, and when we choose to truly love instead of manipulate.

The choices in this phase correspond with many of Erikson's stages of child development—and children need room to learn and grow.[2] The mosaic of our choices soon begins to set a new pattern for our lives. If these choices have been guided by loving and wise counsel, if we have been patient and persistent, and if we have courageously established new healthy patterns, then we may be ready to become emotionally mature.

REFLECTION/DISCUSSION

1. Describe the severity and the nature of your experiences during each of these "turning points":

Too much pain

Tired of the process

Bargaining

Condemned by the family

Vulnerability with someone

Dependence on a friend, counselor, or group leader

Anger at someone who tries to help

Disappointment with new friends

New feelings, new freedom

New boundaries

2. List and contrast some of your old and new perceptions (about yourself, your family, your responsibilities, your feelings, your goals, your motives, etc.) as you continue the healing process.

Old perceptions   **New perceptions**

3. In your own words, explain what it means to:

Identify

Detach

Decide

4. How can you use these "handles" as you go through the process of healing?

5. Paraphrase the following passages:

    Ephesians 4:17–24

    Colossians 3:1–11

    Matthew 10:16

    How do these passages relate to identifying, detaching, and deciding?

[1] Springle, Pat. *Codependency: A Christian Perspective*, Houston and Dallas: Rapha Publishing/Word, Inc., 1990.

[2] Erikson, Eric. *Identity: Youth and Crisis*. New York: Norton, 1968.

18

◆

More Than Surviving

—Pat Springle

Toward the end of her emotional healing process, one woman was still exasperated and desperate. She had faithfully examined the principles presented so far in this book, and she had become able to get "unstuck" in her own emotional and relational progress. "These principles are all fine and good," she told me. "But I need to know what to do about my husband! I need these principles to be translated into clear choices every day—no, every *minute*!"

Most of us are solidly entrenched in painful, dysfunctional relationships with parents, siblings, children, a spouse, or an employer. We were born into some of these relationships; others, we were attracted to for some reason and chose to get more deeply involved. We have replicated sinful and dysfunctional family patterns of behavior. We have been desperate for intimacy and made choices based on that desperation rather than mutual respect and objectivity. For years, our goal has been to survive in these relationships. Real health, real respect, and real love have been fantasies—and shattered dreams.

But if we are willing to focus on our own emotional recovery, we can do far more than just survive. We can grow. Others may not ever change, but we can. We can grieve our losses and wounds. We can give up our demands for justice. Bitterness can change to forgiveness. Our crushed sense of identity can slowly be replaced by a sense of strength and confidence, and the ability to make good choices in relationships.

In fact, the proof that you are growing will be determined in the same relationships which have previously caused you so much pain. If the principles you are learning don't work there, they don't work at all. You may get a fresh perspective from applying these principles to your most difficult *past* relationships, but real growth comes as you learn to apply them in the midst of *current* relationships.

BEING HEALTHY AROUND PAINFUL PEOPLE

Learn to Communicate
Get Objective Input
Establish Boundaries
Find Sources of Refreshment

BEING HEALTHY AROUND PAINFUL PEOPLE

Most people have very unrealistic expectations, so give yourself some breathing room. Don't expect a sudden flash of insight to change a lifetime of patterned reactions into perfect maturity and emotional health. Driven people won't immediately have completely calm responses. Irresponsible people won't automatically handle all of life's details without a hitch. Passive people will still have to struggle to accomplish a surge of initiative.

For a while, you can expect to be deeply discouraged when you don't act perfectly (and surprised when others don't cooperate by acting perfectly in response to your attempts). Your goal should be progress, not perfection.

I heard a leader ask his group, "If you were learning a complicated new sport or board game, you would expect to make some mistakes while you learned, wouldn't you?" People nodded agreeably. He continued, "What if you had some handicap which made the sport or game more difficult? How would that affect your expectations?" Several people commented that they would need to be patient with themselves.

One man observed, "But in my game, I'm not only handicapped. In addition, the other players are telling me I'm stupid and that I'm doing it all wrong."

"Exactly!" the leader said. "That's what each of you experiences in your families or on your job. Give yourself some space. Lower your expectations to slightly less than absolutely perfect every time." At this point, some chuckles were heard from the now understanding group.

The leader concluded, "The harder you try, the more you need support and encouragement from others who have 'been there' and understand what you're going through. It's not your responsibility to do everything to please other people. It is *their* responsibility to respect *your* choices and efforts to relate in a more healthy way. If they don't, it's a reflection on *them*, not *you*."

A regular time and place to "recharge your batteries" will help you maintain realistic expectations. The constant tension in our relationships can quickly drain us. Reading, writing, reflecting, relaxing, and talking to friends can be great help. But we need to make sure we create time for these things.

LEARN TO COMMUNICATE

Many people from dysfunctional families expect others to read their minds. Without expressing themselves, they still want others to know how they *feel*, how they *think*, and what they *want*. But these problematic patterns can be changed as we learn new communication skills, including setting realistic goals, stating opinions clearly, listening, clarifying, and letting others make their own choices.

The first task in learning to communicate more effectively is to set realistic goals for each interaction. This may sound tedious, but it is an invaluable exercise to prevent us from expecting too little or too much from ourselves or the other person. Also, our expectations will probably change as relationships improve or deteriorate.

Once we have a clear idea of what we want to accomplish in each discussion, we can state our opinions and desires clearly and calmly. Perhaps we have a history of being timid and weak, or belligerent and demanding. Now we can learn to calmly state what we want to say with the emphasis we feel is appropriate.

Effective communication also involves learning to listen to the response of the other person. Perhaps he is offended; perhaps he is outraged; perhaps he understands us for the first time. Listening is a difficult task that few of us have learned—especially in regard to those who have deeply hurt us. One good way to listen is to ask follow-up questions that address the deeper reasons and feelings which may not be evident in the person's initial statements.

After listening, we may realize we have been only partially understood, or even misunderstood completely. We can then clarify our opinions, positions, or desires. At this point, we sometimes identify misperceptions or intense feelings that blocked the early stages of the communication process. If so, we can make good progress in the relationship.

Or we may realize that we simply cannot yet come to a satisfactory resolution with the other person. In this case, we can look for as much common ground as possible, and grieve the loss caused by the impasse. But only by continuing to plod through do we ever accomplish positive change. Perhaps later, in another conversation, we can make more progress.

Sometimes the communication process seems to go well, but too often it goes painfully slowly or seems to blow up in our faces. We need to keep in mind that our goal is not to control the other person's behavior, but rather to honor God by our behavior and willingness to let others make their own choices. We may give them a number of options—and remind them of the consequences to each one—but "all we can do is all we can do." As Paul wrote to the believers in Rome, "If possible, so far as it depends on you, be at peace with all men" (Romans 12:18).

GET OBJECTIVE INPUT

Establishing good communication is a tremendously difficult task for many of us. Sometimes we need objective input from a wise friend or counselor, because even as we begin to try to improve the communication in our relationships, we are confronted with many new and frightening choices.

For instance, a lady told me recently, "My brother and sisters want to meet with me. I'm attending a support group at our church and I'm learning and growing, but they don't like the 'new' me."

"Why do you think they want to talk to you?" I asked.

"I'm afraid they want to condemn me and get me to do everything *they* want me to do—like I used to," she answered sadly. "What should I do?"

She was confronted with a new and frightening circumstance, and she sought objective input from me. I told her, "Mary, situations like this can be quite difficult. Your brothers and sisters may be ganging up on you. On the other hand, you may have misinterpreted their intentions. Why not meet with them and ask them their purpose for meeting? If it is what you suspect, you can set your own ground rules for further conversations. One ground rule you might consider is to end the first meeting after their purposes are stated. Then explain that you want to bring an objective counselor to mediate the next conversation. The counselor can assure that the communication remains fair and productive, and he or she can also give you valuable observations about you and your family after the conversation."

Bringing a counselor into the communication process has a couple of drawbacks. One is that the impartial observer might say something you don't want to hear about your role in your family's problems. Another is that it may cost you a little money to have a professional counselor there, though the value far outweighs the cost. (And you might be able to find a pastor with experience in counseling family conflicts to mediate for you.)

More frequently, the objective input you need will come in the form of interaction at a group meeting, a phone call, or a visit with a trusted friend over a cup of coffee. You won't always need a professional, but you do always need objectivity.

Establish Boundaries

As our sense of personal identity grows, we also develop new, healthier boundaries. We determine where our own domain of responsibility and control stops and another person's begins. Our boundaries are determined by our choices, feelings, behaviors, and desires.

In the past we had problems defining boundaries because

we allowed others to control our feelings and actions. Though we did not consciously desire to be manipulated, we desperately wanted to feel the acceptance of others. Similarly, we expected others to make us happy and take care of us. Our identity was shaped by their whims. Our boundaries were trampled again and again. We did and felt what others demanded for so long that we lost touch with what *we* wanted or felt.

But now it is time to take back that power to be responsible for our own lives. We should not hold on to (nor covet) an overbearing, harsh control of others. Rather, we should strive for self-control based on our biblical identity and true humility. (Review Chapter 13.) Reclaiming the power to live our own lives involves the principles already outlined in this book: *identifying* situations where we are allowing others to control us, *detaching* to reflect and examine our choices, and then *deciding* to act on the course we have chosen.

> **W**e *must affirm our own identity, show respect for the other person's right to have an opinion, and open a dialog to build the relationship.*

One very practical element of assuming control of our lives is simply telling others what we want. We should quit trying to read others' minds and making them guess what we are thinking. We must affirm our own identity, show respect for the other person's right to have an opinion, and open a dialog to build the relationship. Of course, we need to have realistic expectations of those who have consistently wounded us. (We need to avoid the pendulum swing from making them guess what we're thinking to making unreasonable demands of them.) If they try to regain control, we can calmly state our desires, listen to what they have to say, reflect, and talk again.

As we define our own identity and establish our own boundaries, we feel less compulsion to transgress the boundaries of others. We make our own choices; we let others make theirs. We experience the consequences of our choices; they experience theirs.

In fact, we sometimes need to give people clear choices of how to relate with us and the consequences of each choice. Then we must follow through on those consequences. A friend related this story:

> James and his wife had three children and a seemingly "happy marriage." One day James walked in and announced, "I haven't loved you for eleven years. I want my freedom. I know we're not supposed to get a divorce, but I'm moving out for a while."
>
> Marianne soon learned that he was not only "moving out"—he was also "moving in" with a friend of theirs. She was devastated, and she offered to change and do whatever she could to make the marriage work. She pleaded with him to return for the sake of the children.
>
> "I can't come back now," he explained. "I've lived in hell with you for so long, I need to be free." Marianne continued to take care of the house. She let James see the children anytime he chose. She was determined to 'bend over backward' to prove her good faith. But after two and a half months, he was still unresponsive.
>
> I told Marianne that her actions and professions of good faith were good, but were not producing repentance in James. We talked about giving him choices and corresponding consequences regarding finances, seeing the children, access to the house, and other issues. If he was unresponsive to one level of consequences, she could go to the next level, but Marianne was unwilling to ask him to choose. Today, a year later, the situation is still the same. James remains unfaithful and free from any consequences which might lead him toward repentance.

Divorce is an issue frequently raised when one person begins to experience emotional health and feels trapped by a controlling, abusive spouse. We do not advise divorce. Rather, if necessary, we suggest a structured separation so that both parties have the freedom to grow and develop healthy responses. Then reconciliation has more opportunity for success. In cases of continued sexual or physical abuse of the spouse or children, we recommend that competent, professional advice be obtained and the guidelines of the person's denomination on separation and divorce be followed.

TOUGHNESS AND FORGIVENESS

Some people whose boundaries have been consistently trampled feel intense bitterness and blame. Others have the opposite response of denial and acquiescence. Neither of these extremes is helpful or productive. But somewhere in the middle is a healthy blend of toughness and forgiveness. Toughness is not the same as harshness or vengeance, nor is forgiveness the same as blindly excusing the offender. This blend of toughness and forgiveness has already been described somewhat, but perhaps another illustration will serve to clarify the point.

Paula had been divorced for several years from her physically and verbally abusive husband, Tom. Under the terms of the divorce, he had rights to see their son, Jason, every other weekend, and he was to pay child support. Knowing her ex's irresponsible character and abusive behavior, Paula feared for her son's emotional well-being and physical safety during those weekends. In addition, Tom had stopped paying Jason's child support *again*—this time for a period of more than two years.

Paula felt overwhelmed by a sense of hopelessness in her situation. She so much dreaded the thought of taking Tom to court again that she allowed him to manipulate her with his "sad" stories of the many reasons he "couldn't afford" to send a check each month. She kept hoping he would magically "grow up" and start to be a responsible father to their son. She also began to feel a "false calm" in regard to Jason's treatment by his dad. *After all, they seemed to be building a good relationship—maybe Tom was beginning to grow in that area, at least!*

As long as Paula stayed in this dream world, everything seemed okay—on the outside anyway! Nobody could see the turmoil that lurked inside of her: the fear of Tom, the shame she felt from her abusive marriage to him, and her feelings of failure. Her subsequent low self-worth would not go away, even though she had been divorced almost six years!

Then Paula had began attending a codependency support group. As she learned and grew, lights came on in regard to her understanding of her relationships—including her past with Tom. She began to develop a new identity, and she realized she had new choices. She also began to separate fantasy from reality, emotional reactions from wise and thought-out decisions, and *her* responsibilities from those that belonged to *others*. She began to deal with the facts of her failed marriage, taking responsibility for her part and relinquishing her responsibility for Tom's behavior (realizing she had no reason to feel ashamed or guilty for what *he* had done).

After one of the weekends with his father, Jason returned home acting very quietly. He didn't want to talk, but Paula knew something had happened. He couldn't sleep well any more and had become extremely fearful of the dark. She also noticed that he was acting very "clingy" and demanding all of her attention. Slowly, over the course of several days, the pieces of the puzzle began to fit together. Paula learned that Tom had gotten on a motorcycle with Jason—neither with helmets—and had driven wildly around town. Jason had been terrified, but Tom had ignored his son's fear. Furthermore, he told Jason that he "shouldn't talk about it to Mom."

Paula was enraged when these facts finally came to light, but what could she do? She said, "In the past I would have been fearful of confronting Tom, but now I'd like to slap him! Yet I know that's not right either. Instead, I was able to talk to him very reasonably about his irresponsibility that particular weekend."

Paula had begun a process she had never experienced before. She chose to begin grieving the deep wound Tom had caused both Jason and herself. Her thoughts and feelings of vengeance were clear and powerful, but she chose to focus instead on God's forgiveness. Though her feelings screamed the opposite, she continued to choose to forgive.

Yet she also knew she had to take action. Paula called a lawyer to see what could be done to protect Jason. The lawyer gave her many options to consider, and she chose the ones which best benefited *Jason*—not the ones which would punish Tom the most. She came to terms with the fact that Tom should be responsible, as the father, to contribute to Jason's welfare by providing child support. She was not responsible for determining whether or not he was capable of following through on the court's decision. She *was* responsible, as Jason's mother, to see that Jason received what the court had ordered on his behalf.

"I should have never married Tom," she told me, "I wasn't concerned at that time about following God's will in my life, and now I'm having to pay the consequences of my wrong decision. But at least I have Jason. He is 'the good' that God has given me from an awful situation."

Paula was learning a lesson in a hard way, but she was making progress.

FIND SOURCES OF REFRESHMENT

Just as a car battery gradually loses its charge when the lights are left on overnight, people who constantly interact with draining or hurtful people need to be recharged regularly—before their battery becomes dead! We all need sources of spiritual and emotional refreshment, and some of us need it more than others. Sadly, some of the ones who need it most are the ones who make the most excuses.

"But I can't! I just don't have time," Mary lamented pitifully, echoing a recurrent refrain of many people.

I wondered whether it was because she *couldn't* or *wouldn't*, so I decided to ask her a few questions. "Mary, who are some people you like to be with?" She listed a few friends.

I asked, "When do you see them?"

"Not often enough!" she retorted.

"When could you see them? Think about your schedule." After a few minutes, Mary realized that she could see people at lunch and on weekends occasionally. It would require some planning and preparation, but it could be done.

Then I asked, "Do you like to read?"

"Not much. Not enough time."

Yet she admitted to reading magazines and ads in the paper, during which time she could be reading selected books instead. "I guess I could spend a little time reading almost every day," she realized.

We continued to talk, and Mary discovered she wasn't as "locked-in" to her schedule and lifestyle as she had assumed. We talked about the need for exercise, sleep, and encouragement. All of these are essential to be able to respond to events in healthy ways. Changes in schedules are not easy to begin or maintain, so we talked about starting slowly, with realistic expectations.

Starting something new is relatively easy, but the real benefits come only through perseverance. Sources of help are available for all of us, and we need to determine a plan that fits our needs.

WEATHER THE STORM

> . . .*They try to manipulate us into staying the way we were (even though they condemned us for being that way, too).*

It's just too easy to get stuck in the healing process, so we must focus on perseverance, not just starting . . . progress, not perfection. Many factors combine to prevent us from overcoming our inertia, keeping us in bondage to old patterns in relationships, feelings, and behaviors. Our schedule doesn't want to budge to make room for exercise, reading, or people. Our families don't like our changes, and they try to manipulate us into staying the way we were (even though they condemned us for being that way, too).

Long-repressed feelings rise to the surface, and we can be overwhelmed by their intensity. New choices threaten us at every turn. And, Satan, the "enemy of our souls" uses all of these factors to accuse us, shame us, and steal our hope. We find our greatest hopes, our greatest joys, our greatest hurts, and our greatest needs in the context of relationships, so our personal interactions will probably be our greatest struggles as we continue to make choices and grow.

We will want to quit many times. We may wish we had never started the whole process. We may lose hope that we can ever be healthy. Such feelings are normal, and though we may need a breather from time to time, we mustn't quit. The stakes are too high and the benefits too great to stop our progress. The Lord is for us.

CHOOSING NEW FRIENDS

Though we can do better than just "survive" our relationships with severely dysfunctional people, we need not limit our social interactions to only those people. We can also choose new friends. In the past, we may have gravitated to certain "types" of people, such as:

- needy people who begged us to fix their problems.
- dominating people who controlled us and made our decisions for us.
- passive people who didn't threaten us in any way.
- wild or passionate people who thrilled us.

. . .We can . . . choose to relate to new friends in relationships based on mutual respect, trust, and honest communication. We no longer need to play games or hide behind facades.

But now, with an improved sense of stability, security, and wisdom, we can make better decisions concerning friendships. We will make the best of the old relationships we choose to keep, but we can also choose to relate to new friends in relationships based on mutual respect, trust, and honest communication. We no longer need to play games or hide behind facades. We can tell the truth, disagree, and still accept others. We can forgive and continue to grow in our relationships instead of being blocked by bitterness.

Relationships have caused our deepest wounds, and relationships will be a vital part of the healing process. Our progress may be long and slow, peppered with spurts of rapid growth, but our goal is to grow to spiritual, emotional, and relational adulthood. The Lord has given us His Word, His Spirit, and His people to encourage and direct us "until we all attain to the unity of the faith, and of the knowledge of the Son of God, to a mature man, to the measure of the stature which belongs to the fulness of Christ" (Ephesians 4:13).

(For much more information on how to thrive in difficult relationships, we recommend H. Norman Wright's book, *How to Get Along with Almost Anyone* [Word, Inc., 1989].)

REFLECTION/DISCUSSION

1. In the past, have you expected others to "read your mind" and know what you want? If so, how has this affected your relationships?

2. Why is it often hard to express what we want, think, and feel?

3. Who can give you objective input on a regular basis? Are you establishing the time to get this input? If not, why not?

4. Why do we need healthy boundaries?

5. When do boundaries become an excuse for selfishness?

6. What is "tough love"?

    Do you need to express "tough love" in your situation? To whom? How? What do you expect to happen?

7. What refreshes you? What do you enjoy?

    Do you feel guilty when you have fun? Why or why not?

8. How do old relationships affect you? Do you need some new friends?

    How can you tell which painful relationships to pursue and which ones to let go?

9. Read Romans 13:8–10. What does it mean to "owe nothing to anyone except to love one another"? Paraphrase this passage in your own words.

19

◆

Becoming an Adult

—Pat Springle

Emotional growth is not unlike physical growth, in that we need to pass through a number of various stages before reaching maturity. The stages of physical growth are easily identified. It's simple enough to tell a toddler from an adolescent from a full-grown adult. But determining one's level of emotional maturity is more complicated.

People tend to think they are farther along than they actually are. Many believe they have completed the process of emotional maturity, when they have only begun. When emotional adolescence is described to people who are just beginning the healing process, they almost invariably conclude that's the stage of growth they are in. (In other words people who suppose they are adults are willing to admit that they are adolescents, when they are actually toddlers.) They relate to the description of mood swings, experimentation, enthusiasm, depression, new friends, risks, and changes. Yet most of these adolescent traits are also quite common in toddlers! Arrival at a true adolescent stage comes only after many hurdles have been cleared and thousands of tough decisions have been made.

Even after many cycles of realization, grief, responsibility, and (to some degree) healing, most people still have somewhat reactionary, black-or-white tendencies. Expanding boundaries, new freedom of expression, and burgeoning confidence may, in fact, create additional conflict.

Like the high school years, emotional adolescence is full of contradictions—wounds and healing, hurts and strengths, progress and regression, wins and losses. But we continue to experiment and explore new choices, and we form a clearer concept of who we are and how we want to relate to others. As these concepts stabilize and become clear, we move toward adulthood.

DEVELOP A NEW IDENTITY

The more we replace our torn-down defense mechanisms with the love and grace of God, the less we miss our protective facades. In early adolescence, we play games to impress people and win approval, but later we abhor those games and the phoniness in our relationships. We want reality (though we're not exactly sure what reality is!). Confidence and self-acceptance gradually replace our fear, protection, hiding, compensating, and the things we do to impress others.

> *"I don't have to be everything to everybody anymore."*

"I don't have to be everything to everybody anymore," one man stated. "I'm learning that I can accept my strengths without being prideful and my weaknesses without being ashamed."

A growing sense of identity results from making our own choices about goals, desires, feelings, behaviors, and relationships. As we grow, we learn to see more options in every situation.

A woman told me, "I can't believe how 'locked-in' I used to feel. I either had to do what my husband wanted—or else. That wasn't much of a choice! Now I see that I have lots of choices. I can detach and feel and think. Then there are options of what I want to say or do, and how and when I want to say or do them. I never knew I was so narrow before!"

Our new identity also clarifies our motivations. Fear, hatred, shame, and craving are gradually supplanted by better motivations and clearer priorities. We realize that we can choose only a few things that are truly important. We can't do everything. But our new identity enables us to make those tough choices out of love, honor, and duty instead of guilt and fear.

The apostle Paul, after describing the love of God and the believer's identity in Christ, encourages the Ephesian Christians to act on that new identity: "I, therefore, the prisoner of the Lord, entreat you to walk in a manner worthy of the calling with which you have been called" (Ephesians 4:1).

The three chapters of Ephesians that follow this challenge are filled with clarifications of relationships and admonitions to obedience. The motivation of the first three chapters becomes the platform for Christian behavior described in the last three. Our motivation will not be 100 percent pure until we see God "face to face" (1 Corinthians 13:12). But in the meantime, the closer we get to genuine love in our relationships, the farther away from the oppressive motivation of pure guilt we are carried.

REALISTIC EXPECTATIONS

As we mature emotionally, our expectations become more realistic. At the beginning of the process we are surprised each time we go through a new cycle and experience a deeper level of pain. Maturity, however, teaches us that we have many, many layers to deal with. We are no longer shocked to find that our wounds are deeper, our behaviors more dysfunctional, and our perception more blinded than we previously thought.

We develop realistic expectations in relationships and establish healthy boundaries. Pete described his experience:

> For years I let my parents and my sister have whatever they wanted. When I tried to be myself I either felt terribly guilty, was told I was 'selfish,' or both." He described years of being abused. His drug addict sister had taken his car and a lot of his money.

Finally, I realized that enough was enough! I had thought I was awful if I didn't give them everything they demanded. I was depressed, angry, and broken. Something had to change. After being in counseling for a while, I realized that I didn't know the first thing about love and respect. I was all mixed up. As my confidence grew, I confronted them—my sister first, then my parents. I told them that I felt hurt and that I wanted a better relationship with them. I said, "I don't demand that you treat me with love, like a brother or a son. I only ask that you treat me with a little respect—like a person." I gave them a choice of whether they wanted to build a relationship with me on that basis: respect and honesty. Maybe it would grow to be love, who knows? But I was not willing to have the kind of relationship we used to have.

An aspect of being realistic is facing the fact that some people are quite threatening to us. A spouse, child, parent, or close friend can attack us incessantly, and we need to be prepared when we interact with them. In the early stages of our development, we probably vacillated between continuing to give in to their control and reacting harshly against it. As progress continued, we learned to detach, reflect, and become more objective. We saw more options for how to respond. We became less compulsive to make the other person change, and we started preparing for our communications with others.

Rob told our group about his need to be prepared when he talked to his dad: "Every time he saw me coming, he chewed me out. No matter what I had done, it was wrong. I had to brace myself every time I saw him or even talked on the phone. The first few times I talked to him after completing my treatment, I wrote pages of notes to prepare myself to talk to him. I was ready for him, too. I mean, who wants to go into a lion's den naked, with A-1 Steak Sauce smeared all over his body?!"

Preparation requires work. It requires that we reflect on old wounds and new choices. Nothing can guarantee success, but preparation gives us confidence to act on our new identity and take new, confident strides in our journey.

Realistic expectations should also affect our friendships. Many of us have been compulsively driven toward certain people, while we hide from others. As we mature, we realize that we don't need everybody, but we do need a few close friends.

Through emotional adolescence and into emotional adulthood, we choose people to be our closest friends. By trial and error we discover that many people are superficial and don't understand our new perceptions. But a few do. These cherished individuals are rare. We value their contribution to our lives.

We also learn to live with ambiguities. Black-or-white, all-or-nothing thinking fades as we realize that most of life is found in the enormous, harder-to-handle dimension of gray. To be sure, there are still standards of right and wrong, but fewer and fewer issues or relationships can be contained in either of these extremes. Increased confidence and a stronger sense of identity enable us to be less threatened by these ambiguities. We no longer have to "nail down" the right and wrong of every issue. We learn to understand and even empathize with those who disagree with us.

We become more comfortable with ourselves and with life. Those who have coped by being intense are more calm. Those who have coped by withdrawing, using drugs, or being depressed are motivated to build and grow. We become more focused on the few important things in life, and more realistic in our expectations.

A NEW APPRECIATION FOR GOD

If we have been able to differentiate the love of God from the "love" of those who have hurt us, perhaps we experienced His comfort early in the healing process. But many others need more time to discover that God is not just like the offenders. Trusting Him is a great threat which takes courage to begin and tenacity to continue.

Despair gives way to hope that God will come through—not necessarily in the way we want Him to—but in His way and His timing.

Throughout the process, "Why?" becomes a common question. "God, why did You let this happen to me? If You loved me it wouldn't have happened." Tough questions come from a broken heart, and as we express our true feelings to God, we learn to experience His comfort. Healing gives us better perspective. Despair gives way to hope that God will come through—not necessarily in the way we want Him to—but in His way and His timing.

David experienced deep despair, and he openly expressed his discouragement to the Lord. He wrote: "I would have despaired unless I had believed that I would see the goodness of the Lord in the land of the living" (Psalms 27:13). Without seeing an answer in sight, he could still trust the goodness and sovereignty of God. And he waited for God, expecting Him to answer: "Wait for the Lord; be strong, and let your heart take courage; yes, wait for the Lord" (Psalms 27:14).

Trust is the foundation of our relationship with God. As we realize that He is trustworthy, we experience more of His peace. We no longer need to know all the answers because we are assured that at least *He* understands even if *we* don't.

PACING THE JOURNEY

We are tempted to try to go through the process of emotional healing very quickly—or not at all. The prospect of a slow, arduous pace is abhorrent to us. We need to have patience with ourselves and with God. Healing is a slow process. Deep wounds require a lot of time and attention. The journey is a long one.

Between my junior and senior years in college, my friend Graham and I headed West to camp and hike. After a stop at the Piggly Wiggley, for such health food as Vienna sausages, instant coffee, and canned peas, we took off. We spent the first night in his grandmother's driveway in Arkansas. (We got there too late to wake her up.) We had a misadventure or two on the highway in Oklahoma, and a memorable breakfast at a diner near Gallup, New Mexico, where I sat next to the Bunny Bread truck driver. (I would have given $10 for his shirt with the huge embroidered smiling rabbit on it, but we were on a tight budget.) Finally we pulled in at our first major destination—the south rim of the Grand Canyon.

We set up our tent just before a tremendous thunderstorm (Can you say "mud"?), and we met a ranger who gave us his advice on trying to hike all the way down and back in one day: "It's a tough climb back out." As Graham and I left the ranger station, we looked at each other and smiled. Graham said what both of us were thinking, "I'll bet he tells everybody that story to keep the little old ladies out of trouble."

We had a great meal of—well, I've already mentioned our culinary selections—and got a good night's sleep. After a breakfast just like supper the night before, we headed for the trail—all 17 miles of it, down and back. The morning was gorgeous, cool, and cloudless. We started down amid gnarled pines, cactus, and layers of rock which showed every geologic age Graham could remember from his class last quarter. About a mile down, I said, "Why don't we hike *up* the trail for a hundred yards or so to see what it'll be like later today?"

We trudged a few steps and each of us knew what the other wasn't saying, *The ranger was right!* But neither of us said a word except, "Okay, that's good, let's go on down." We silently made the choice to keep going, but now we knew we were going to have to strain to get back to our starting point.

We passed Indian Gardens at about 9:30 and entered the inner canyon about an hour later. After six miles or so, we started getting tired. We tried to keep a steady pace because if we walked too fast, we might fall. But if we took it too slow, we might not get out that day.

We reached the river just in time to eat our lunch of—well, you know. After a hoot and a yell at a raftload of people going by, we started back. Only a few hundred yards up, I thought, *Good grief! It was hard going uphill this morning, but this is awful!* Graham had worked inside at a bank all summer, and without much physical stamina, he needed to rest pretty soon. When we got going again, it wasn't long before we needed another rest.

It was now early afternoon and about 120 degrees in the inner canyon. As we rested for the 7,323rd time during our first mile back up, a mule-riding party came by. I thought about hitting one of the tourists in the head with a rock and stealing his mule, but it didn't seem to be the loving, Christ-like thing to do. So we kept walking.

After eight months (okay, it was four hours—but it seemed a lot longer!) we struggled into Indian Gardens. I wish I had a dime for every time Graham and I had thought, *We never should have done this,* or *We should have listened to the ranger,* but neither of us said much. Pride, you know.

The sun went down with the top of the canyon nowhere in sight. Graham had a cramp in his leg. Some crazy guy from UCLA joined us. He thought yodeling in the canyons was the most fun he'd ever had—for *him* anyway!

After another rest we set out again. *Keep going. . . . We'll make it. . . . Boy, won't it be great to get to the top?* Every step we took became a choice to keep going or stop. Spontaneity had disappeared hours ago. Now we relied on sheer willpower and whatever shreds of strength we could muster.

At 10:30 that night, Graham and I crawled out of the Grand Canyon like two beat-up snakes. Forget supper.

"I'm not hungry. You?"

Graham grunted, "Nah."

We got back to the tent and flopped down, fully clothed, boots on, no brain waves, only pain. But we had made it! The next day, we'd be really glad. For the rest of our lives we could talk about this experience. Many times on the way up it hadn't seemed worth it—but it was.

"I've been in the healing process a long time, but I'm so glad to be where I am today.

A friend of mine recently told me, "I've been in the healing process a long time, but I'm so glad to be where I am today. If I never progress one more step, that's okay. It's worth it."

Many of us begin the process out of desperation. We continue through many, many grueling, exciting, confusing times. Sometimes we get so tired that we can hardly go on. Yet with courage and perseverance, we will be able to look back some day and say, "It was worth it."

REFLECTION/DISCUSSION

1. Contrast your old sense of identity with your new one by completing these statements:

    I was . . .

I am . . .

2. Read the first three chapters of Ephesians and list every characteristic of your identity in Christ.

3. How do you feel about this description of yourself?

4. Why is it so important to have realistic expectations of the healing process?

5. As a result of reading this book, has your view of God been affected? If so, how?

6. Complete these statements:

    Over the next several months I need to . . .

    God needs to help me by . . .

    I expect . . .

Appendix

◆

Using *Getting Unstuck* in Groups

Getting Unstuck is designed to be used both individually and in groups. In fact, the combination of individual reading and reflection combined with group interaction is most helpful.

The book can be used as a supplement to support group material. If the facilitator realizes that the group members are resistant and having difficulty making progress, he or she may use *Getting Unstuck* for a few weeks to stimulate reflection, discussion, and steps forward.

In the context of an ongoing support group, you may want to have the group focus on a few particular chapters in the book, or you can study the entire book as a 13-week hiatus from the usual material.

Quarterly growth groups can also effectively use *Getting Unstuck.* Many churches use these groups to get people more in touch with relational, emotional, and spiritual hurts and needs. After a few quarters, many groups seem to "bog down." Some people may be ready and willing to make real progress, but others are hesitant. *Getting Unstuck* can be useful in helping the group members to understand their hesitancy and give them wisdom and courage to keep going in their recovery process.

Growth groups which have used *The Search for Significance* and *Codependency: A Christian Perspective* are usually ready for a series using *Getting Unstuck*.

The question at the end of each chapter will aid reflection and discussion. The best method, obviously, is for group members to read and answer the questions before they come to the group. Then, discussions will be more meaningful.

In either support groups or growth groups, we recommend the following 13-week format:

Week 1 .... Chapters 1 and 2
Week 2 .... Chapter 3
Week 3 .... Chapter 4
Week 4 .... Chapter 5
Week 5 .... Chapter 6
Week 6 .... Chapter 7
Week 7 .... Chapter 8
Week 8 .... Chapters 9 and 10
Week 9 .... Chapter 11
Week 10 .... Chapters 12 and 13
Week 11 .... Chapters 14 and 15
Week 12 .... Chapters 16 and 17
Week 13 .... Chapters 18 and 19

For insights about asking good questions, promoting inter-action, avoiding cross-talk, and other practical ideas, order *Rapha's Handbook for Group Leaders*. Send $5.00 with your name and address to:

Rapha, Inc.
8876 Gulf Freeway, Suite 340
Houston, Texas 77017

Also, if you have problems or questions about your group, or if someone in your group has severe problems and you need to find clinical help, call the Small Group Hotline at 1 (800) 383-HOPE.

"ADULT CHILDREN" GROUPS

This book would also be ideal for a newly formed group of Adult Children of Alcoholics, Adult Children of Divorce, Adult Children of Dysfunctional Families, etc. Sharing experiences with a small group of others who understand your situation is one of the most effective ways of getting unstuck in your journey to emotional healing.

If you have any questions about using this book in your group, please call Rapha's Group Leaders' Hotline at 1 (800) 383-HOPE.

ROBERT S. McGEE is a professional counselor and lecturer who has helped thousands of people experience the love and acceptance of Jesus Christ. He is also the Founder and President of Rapha, a nationally recognized health care organization that provides in-house care with a Christ-centered perspective for adults and adolescents suffering with psychiatric and substance abuse problems. The truths presented in his book, *The Search for Significance*, form the foundational cornerstones that provide the balance of spiritual and clinical therapy in the Rapha Treatment Centers program.

He is also the author of *Discipline with Love* and co-author of several books, including *Rapha's 12-Step Program for Overcoming Chemical Dependency*, *Rapha's 12-Step Program for Overcoming Eating Disorders*, *Renew: Hope for Victims of Sexual Abuse*, *Bitterness*, and *Your Parents and You*.

PAT SPRINGLE is Senior Vice President, Church and Family Resources, for Rapha. He served on the staff of Campus Crusade for Christ for 18 years, 11 years as their Texas area director. Pat lives in Houston with his wife, Joyce, and his two children, Catherine and Taylor. He is the author or coauthor of several books, including *Rapha's 12-Step Program for Overcoming Codependency*, *Bitterness*, *Close Enough to Care*, and *Codependency: A Christian Perspective*.